ROSS, Elizabeth Dale. **The kindergarten crusade: the establishment of preschool education in the United States.** Ohio University, 1976. 120p bibl index 75-36986. 8.50 ISBN 0-8214-0206-4; 4.25 pa ISBN 0-8214-0228-5

A remarkable piece of scholarship. The history of the kindergarten in the U.S. is interestingly traced from its origins as a private preschool innovation in 1860 through its general acceptance in most urban public schools by 1914. The influence of Froebel's kindergarten, developed in Germany during the 1830s and '40s, upon U.S. programs is made clear, as is the influence which the U.S. kindergartens have had on primary school education in the U.S. Quotes and illustrative anecdotes are used effectively. Ross's bibliographic essay is impressive. She has used most of the primary sources available throughout the U.S. and has relied heavily on Froebel's books, essays, and letters. Also included are lists of biographies; periodicals, bulletins, and journals; annual reports; and books that treat particular aspects of the kindergarten movement. Indexing is thorough. A readable, well-researched account of the development of kindergartens in the U.S. has been long overdue. Highly recommended for both undergraduate and graduate libraries that serve early childhood or elementary education programs.

Elizabeth D. Ross has taught at Howard University and the State University of New York College at Buffalo. She is the mother of two young children.

THE KINDERGARTEN CRUSADE:
THE ESTABLISHMENT OF
PRESCHOOL EDUCATION
IN THE UNITED STATES

by
Elizabeth Dale Ross

Ohio University Press
Athens, Ohio

CONTENTS

PREFACE

This book traces the history of the kindergarten in the United States from its origins as a private preschool educational innovation around 1860 through its general acceptance in most urban public school systems by 1914. A group of remarkably liberated and well-educated women championed the cause of early childhood education in these decades. Their crusade to establish kindergartens in the United States flourished and matured in the late nineteenth and early twentieth centuries, making several lasting contributions to American education and social reform.

The idea of the kindergarten was originated by Friedrich Froebel in Germany in the 1830's and 1840's. Devised as a preschool curriculum for three to seven year old children, the kindergarten was a system of intellectual, moral, and physical education which reflected pedagogical principles that were ordinarily considered foolish and extreme in the middle of the nineteenth century; namely, that children's play was significant and that the curriculum should be based on children's interests and needs.

In the 1860's, Froebel's concepts of the kindergarten began to attract the attention of several well-known American educators. They recognized that his philosophy embodied significant principles of child development and as a result of their interest several private kindergartens were opened in the United States. In the following decade, a group of pedagogically-minded reformers worked to organize kindergartens in urban ghetto areas for children who otherwise would be deprived of the opportunity. The idea spread enthusiastically, and philanthropic kindergarten associations grew up in cities of all sizes. These organizations did not limit their activities to charity work; they also endeavored to have kindergartens incorporated into the public school systems, a goal reached in most major cities by the first quarter of the twentieth century.

The kindergarten contributed to American educational reform in several ways. During the latter part of the nineteenth century, experts in the field of child study, such as John Dewey and Francis Parker, freely acknowledged their intellectual debts to Froebel. Many of the basic tenets of their "new" or "progressive" education lay deeply imbedded in kindergarten theory and practice. In addition, courses in kindergartening were often among the most exciting, innovative offerings at even the best normal schools and teachers' colleges. While the kindergarten lost some of its old identity and social reform functions when it became part of the public school system, its ideas and material helped change the rigid formalism and discipline of the primary grades.

Today, psychologists, sociologists, educators, parents, and other concerned persons are still grappling with the basic issues of early childhood education raised by kindergartners a century ago. Many are returning to the earlier positions on such matters as conceptual learning through play, the efficacy of teaching reading to preschool children, the effectiveness of compensatory education, and the relationship between families, children, and schools.

ACKNOWLEDGEMENTS

Several people contributed invaluable assistance during the preparation of this manuscript. I especially want to thank Professor Timothy L. Smith of Johns Hopkins University for his insightful questioning, advice, and encouragement. I would also like to express my appreciation to all those who read this work and offered helpful criticism and comments at various points along the way, particularly Professor Charles Biebel of the University of New Mexico; Professor W. Bruce Leslie of the State University College of New York at Brockport; Professor Charles Burgess of the University of Washington; Professor Shirley N. Winters of Hofstra University; and Professor George Woytanowitz of Boston College.

Among the numerous archivists who facilitated my research are Betty Mirhaba at the Association for Childhood Education International; Kathleen Jacklin at the Collection of Regional History and University Archives at Cornell University; and Frances H. Stadler at the Missouri Historical Society.

CHAPTER I

THE EARLY KINDERGARTEN EXPERIENCE IN AMERICA

The introduction of the kindergarten in the United States in the 1850's marked a radically new approach to education in America. Originated by Friedrich Froebel in Germany twenty years earlier, the kindergarten provided a child-centered, preschool curriculum for three to seven year old children that aimed at unfolding the child's physical, intellectual, and moral nature with balanced emphasis on each of them. Froebel alleged that traditional schools concentrated too heavily on developing the intellect through reading, writing, and memorizing. Although he was concerned with schools in Germany, he might have levelled such criticism equally as well at schools in the United States of that period or perhaps anywhere in Europe for that matter. In the belief that one phase of education must build on the child's previous development, Froebel chose to concentrate his theory of kindergarten education on preschool children who he thought needed a larger social group than the family. In contrast to the formality of existing schools, Froebel designed his program on the premise that play was the most natural and educational activity for a young child, and he translated what was ordinarily considered work into the child's realm of play, a revolutionary idea for his time.

It was through the activities of Elizabeth Palmer Peabody, one of the earliest and most active American kindergarten pioneers, that Froebel's ideas were gradually recognized in America. Elizabeth was

1

born near Boston in 1804 to parents of modest means and grew up along with her younger brothers and sisters in a warm family environment. Her mother, who conducted a school in Salem and whose philosophy instinctively reflected Froebel's ideas of child development although she had never heard of him, influenced Elizabeth keenly. Her father also played a significant role during her formative years—for example, she became sensitized to the needs of the poor as a result of accompanying him on visits to local almshouses. These lasting impressions ultimately influenced her own philosophical ideas on preschool education.

Peabody's long teaching career began at the age of sixteen and encompassed a wide variety of pedagogical experiences. She briefly ran her own school in Boston; at the same time she was learning Greek under the tutelage of the young Ralph Waldo Emerson. For two years she served as a governess and a tutor in Maine and then returned to open a school in Brookline with her sister Mary. William Ellery Channing entrusted his only daughter to their care, and through conferences about the daughter's education, Elizabeth became an intimate associate of the Channings. She later acted as Bronson Alcott's assistant in his controversial Temple School. Elizabeth became fast friends with many young intellectuals, reformers, and educators of the period. Two of them, Horace Mann and Nathaniel Hawthorne, later married her sisters Mary and Sophia. Elizabeth's intellectual capacity, her reading, thinking, resourceful personality, and relationships with those who formed the Transcendental Club in 1837 kept her in the forefront of avant-garde Boston literary and intellectual circles.[1]

Elizabeth Peabody first heard about the kindergarten system in 1859 from Margarethe Meyer Schurz at the Boston home of a mutual friend. At this meeting, Peabody was fascinated as Margarethe Schurz explained some of Friedrich Froebel's precepts and described her own experiences in kindergartening. She had been trained by Froebel in Germany and had set up a small, private, German-speaking kindergarten for family and friends in Watertown, Wisconsin, in 1856. She followed up the conversation by sending Peabody the preface to Froebel's *Education of Man*, available at that time only in the original German. With characteristic motivation and energy, Peabody read it and, basing her understanding of Froebel's philosophy on what she had heard and read, she opened a kindergarten in Boston in 1860.

2

Peabody was an enthusiastic convert. She lectured on the subject of kindergartening to a growing audience, and with the collaboration of her sister, Mary Mann, she published a book called *Kindergarten Guide*. The lectures were successful in introducing people to Froebel's ideas; the book sold many copies; and the kindergarten survived financially. Peabody, however, began to suspect the shallowness of her ventures. Fearing the inadequacy of her preparation and doubting whether her kindergarten was actually what Froebel had intended, she closed it in 1867 and travelled to Germany to learn more about Froebel's life and philosophy.[2]

She learned that Friedrich Froebel had opened his first kindergarten in Blankenburg in 1837. Earlier, he had taught at the Model School of Frankfurt-on-the-Main. Unhappy with the necessity of clockwork-like precision needed in teaching at a large institution, however, he left after a brief stay. His own ideas about education "called only for ready senses and awakened intellect." He felt that in the Model School's environment, vitality and activity too easily stiffened into "bony rigidity."[3] After participating in several other educational enterprises, including private tutoring and his own school at Keilhau, Froebel finally devoted all his energies to developing his kindergarten idea at Blankenburg.

Froebel's kindergarten philosophy had to be disentangled from his rambling, obscure, and often incoherent writing style to be understood.* The Baroness Marenholtz-Bulow, his dear friend and chief disciple, remarked that although Froebel's articulation of his own ideas was as poor as his literary talent, observers who watched him in action with children praised his work overwhelmingly. Even the most antagonistic visitors, dragooned by the Baroness to observe Froebel conduct a kindergarten, were completely won over to the virtues of his system. Often, when meeting new people, or when he could not communicate satisfactorily, Froebel would ask the Baroness to speak for him, since she understood his ideas thoroughly.**

* Froebel showed his awareness of this problem in a letter to a friend asking him to correct a draft of an essay, commenting that he knew that his style "was not readily intelligible to all." Friedrich Froebel to Von Arnswald, Keilhau, October 30, 1847, in Arnold Heinemann, editor, *Froebel's Letters* (Boston: Lothrop, Lee & Shepard Co., 1893).

** In Baroness Marenholtz-Bulow, *Reminiscences of Friedrich Froebel*, Mary Mann, translator (New York: C.T.Dillingham, 1877), 18-19, the Baroness gave a colorful account of the evening that Froebel attended a formal dinner with the Duchess Ida of Marienthal with the intention of petitioning her husband to give him a building for his school. Dressed in a formal tuxedo provided for him by the Baroness

3

Froebel's thoughts on religion pervaded his entire philosophy. According to him, all life was based on what he called the eternal law of unity, that is, the interconnection of all things in life. God was the supreme or "Divine Unity" and the source of all subsequent unity. Education, in the most general sense, was the process of leading man to a conscious appreciation of those principles. Froebel spoke of religion in a broad, non-sectarian sense, and he referred frequently to the concept of Christian love, meaning love which was a conscious reflection of the divine origin of man. He wanted the child to learn to appreciate God through observation, reflection, and activity, not through dogmatic religious teaching.[4]

Although man's spiritual development had the highest priority in Froebel's pedagogy, he envisioned its cultivation in harmony with physical and intellectual growth. Froebel himself felt that his emphasis upon interconnection and unity which stemmed from his view of Divine Unity distinguished his educational system from all others. Even at Pestalozzi's school in Yverdon, where Froebel was an admiring visitor, he found each subject efficiently taught, but fragmented and too mechanical. While Pestalozzi rested his innovative system on the principle of observation, Froebel combined observation with actual doing, thereby allowing the child to develop his abilities and express his own creative impulses.[5]

One of Froebel's most significant contributions to education was his appreciation of the educative value of play. During childhood, he said, play was "never trivial," but rather "serious and deeply significant." He urged parents to cherish and encourage it, since "in his free choice of play a child reveals the future life of his mind to anyone who has insight into human nature." In fact, he regarded play as "the highest level of child development."[6] Consequently, in the curriculum that Froebel devised for the kindergarten, he sought to help the child unfold his abilities by directing his playing. In the process, he gradually wanted to lead the joy the child felt in playing to his attitudes toward work and the rest of school activities.[7]

Elizabeth Peabody found all these ideas consonant with her own and similar to the basis of her teaching at Alcott's Temple School. What she welcomed most in Froebel was that he had worked his ideas into a precise system. Basing his kindergarten program on de-

Marenholtz, Froebel came to dinner with farm manure on his boots. The odor in the room was unpleasant, and the Duchess opened a window. Finally the Baroness figured out the source of the problem, and all laughed, including Froebel.

4

veloping the child's physical, intellectual, and moral nature, Froebel devised three categories: (1) the gifts or playthings; (2) the occupations or handiwork activities; and (3) the songs, games, stories, and gardening. Together, these activities restricted the child's complete freedom, yet still gave him outlets for self-expression, offered the opportunity to develop manual dexterity, and taught him about geometric as well as social and natural relationships.

The "gifts" were an intrinsic part of Froebel's system. He arranged them in a logical geometric sequence. The first gift was the ball, the earliest and most important plaything of the child. He received it first in the nursery, then in the kindergarten where he would use it again. In playing with the ball with his mother or nurse, Froebel's idea was that the child developed his sense of observation and learned such concepts as presence, absence, return, seeking, finding, clasping, rolling, sliding, and falling. There was a series of six balls conveying the entire color spectrum: red, blue, yellow, green, purple, and orange. Froebel pointed out that although the very young child might be physically helpless, he was very aware of his immediate environment and learned much more than adults supposed. However, to Froebel, the greatest significance of the ball was its physical embodiment of his concept of unity: the three-dimensional circle was the purest of forms. Although it was representative of all objects, both animate and inanimate, it maintained its own form. Froebel's insistence that the child become aware of these mystical relationships was difficult to convey even to the teacher: he felt that the child would see a parallel between his own inner unity, i.e., interconnections within himself, and that of the ball. Thus, the ball would serve as a mirror image to the child.[8]

The second gift, comprising a wooden sphere, cube, and cylinder, represented variety, contrast, and synthesis, or in Hegelian terms, thesis, antithesis, and synthesis. The geometrical properties of the cube, particularly its corners, were in clear contrast to the round sameness of the sphere, with which the child was already familiar from his observation of the ball. As the child played with each object, he learned to express verbally the distinguishing qualities of the forms; and the introduction of the cylinder, which combined the three-dimensional roundness of the sphere with the edges of the cubes, resolved the contrast.

The third through sixth gifts, the building gifts, moved to more creative activities. The third was a cube divided into eight smaller

5

cubes; the fourth, a two-inch cube divided into eight oblong blocks; and the fifth and sixth, cubes divided even more intricately. As in the first two gifts, the child observed the concept of unity, but now he could also clearly see the relationship of dependence between the parts and the whole. Using these cubes, he could express himself by dismantling them and arranging the parts to form different wholes. These gifts allowed the child much freedom of imagination, because although the teacher, known as a kindergartner, guided a portion of the child's building, she allowed him to express his own ideas the rest of the time.

With the seventh gift, a one-inch square and four different triangles made of very thin pieces of colored wood, the gifts moved from the realm of solids to that of the plane. The eighth and ninth gifts were small sticks of varying lengths and wire rings and half rings of different sizes. These two gifts together provided the child with infinite possibilities for design. Finally, the tenth gift was any object which symbolized a point, such as a seed or a pebble. Arranged in logical geometric sequence and presented to the child in that order, Froebel believed that the ten gifts would guide the child to the relationship of the whole to its parts.

The second aspect of Froebel's system, the occupations, began after the tenth gift had been presented and used, and proceeded to teach the child to work with a variety of solid forms and textures. In perforating heavy paper with a long needle, the child made geometric designs or anything else that appealed to him. Other handiwork included: sewing with brightly-colored wool or embroidering in silk; drawing, both outline and freehand work; paper twisting; weaving colored strips of paper; paper cutting; paper folding; and finally clay modelling, which had a multitude of creative possibilities. Thus, the order of the gifts and occupations started with the most basic geometric solid forms, broke them down into components, and returned finally to the solid.

Froebel substituted songs, games, stories, conversations, and gardening, comprising the ·last part of the kindergarten system, for the reading, writing, and other traditional school activities. The songs and games made it necessary for the child to make an individual contribution to the functioning of the group. He also thought that they provided musical and rhythmic training as well as ethical lessons. The material in Froebel's *Mutter Und Köse Lieder*, a collection of games and songs for a mother or kindergartner to play

6

with the child, when combined with similar ones described in the *Pedagogics of the Kindergarten,* was intended to provide ample opportunity for the child's social and personal development. Baroness Marenholtz, in her *Reminiscences,* declared that the main purpose of all the plays was the child's realization of himself as an integral member of a group. Thus in the now familiar game "Did You Ever See a Lassie?" one child goes into the center of the circle, makes a rhythmic movement, and the others imitate him, permitting him to see himself reflected in the actions of the group.[9]

Froebel also envisioned his kindergartens in a rural environment where the children would live with and learn from nature. This fact is important to note, since later kindergartens in the United States existed predominantly in large urban centers where pupils and teachers did not have the opportunity to have the kinds of experiences Froebel deemed essential. He, for example, assumed that each child would tend his own small garden and in doing so would see a similar image to his own development. Some urban kindergartners substituted an activity such as each child planting a seed in the classroom, while other classes were fortunate enough to have rooftop gardens. Froebel's romanticism about the unity and goodness in nature which he felt the child capable of comprehending and reflecting can be summed up in his contention that: "A child who . . . seeks out flowers, cares for them, and protects them . . . can never become a base child or a wicked man."[10]

In all ways, Froebel designed his system and kindergarten activity to give each child the opportunity to conceptualize relationships independently; he understood that the child was creative and productive, not merely receptive. In the kindergarten, the child learned through activity. He learned about geometric forms, about number, expression, beauty, and both social and intellectual relationships, as a result of his own behavior and curiosity. With marked insight, Froebel recognized that real education could only occur when the child puzzled things out for himself.[11]

Finally, Froebel realized the obviously crucial role of the teacher, the kindergartner; if she were ill-trained or of the wrong temperament and attitude, the undertaking would involve no more than random play. He hoped to release the child from the straitjacket of traditional education and to prescribe a system that would promote the development of each individual; and for his allies and helpers he looked to women to execute his idea. The kindergartner had to

7

embody the ideals of motherhood, and thus he often told Baroness Marenholtz that his system needed the devotion of not only sensitive but "intellectually active women."[12] He sought to train such women as kindergarten teachers.

In 1848, four years before Froebel's death, the Prussian authorities banned the kindergarten as subversive. Froebel's contemporaries felt that he had been mistakenly identified with the political activism of his radical nephew. Heartbroken, the German educator often expressed the hope that the United States might be more receptive to his ideas. His close friend, Madame Marenholtz, spent several years after his death travelling around Europe spreading his ideas in England, Holland, France, Switzerland, and Italy. A few former pupils trained by Froebel or his wife emigrated to the United States during the 1860's and 1870's and taught their own training courses for people interested in becoming kindergartners. Several of them, like Maria Boelte and Emma Marwedel, were encouraged to come by Elizabeth Peabody during her trip abroad in 1867-68.[13]

Elizabeth Peabody returned to the United States after studying and absorbing Froebelian thought and philosophy. Already mature in years, she gave up the notion of practical classroom work and channeled her energies into promoting kindergartens as she then understood them. She repudiated her earlier book and kindergarten, describing the latter as having been "only the old primary school, ameliorated by a mixture of infant plays."[14] In public lectures, in articles, in personal correspondence, and in the *Kindergarten Messenger*, a journal she published for several years, she dwelt upon such Froebelian concepts as the innocence of children and spirit of God in them; religious nurture rather than religious dogma; the sinfulness of breaking a child's will; respect for the child as an individual; the evaluation of children as they were in the kindergarten, not as they might be when grown up; cultivating children rather than drilling them, regarding the latter procedure as appropriate only to "insensate stone;" and about the natural wildness of children during certain games and the importance of keeping the application of adult restraint within "reasonable limits."[15]

She particularly stressed the necessity of maintaining high standards in training kindergarten teachers, even when a crucial shortage of teachers existed in the early years of the movement. Kindergartening, she held, was both "a vocation from on high" and "the perfect development of womanliness." A kindergartner needed to be well-educated, imaginative, and refined, although not necessarily from a wealthy home. She must be truly religious and, in Peabody's terms, ultimately committed to cultivating a heaven on earth. In pursuing this "vocation from on high," Peabody insisted without exception upon regular, thorough training. She endeavored to dispel the myth that it was easier to teach three- and four-year-old children than fifteen-year-old children, emphasizing that the former task was not only more difficult but more critical. Responding to a letter from a friend's daughter seeking advice, Peabody told her not to take an abbreviated course but a proper two-year one, if she "ever wished to take the name of kindergartner."[16]

Writing and publishing the *Kindergarten Messenger* gave Elizabeth Peabody the leverage she needed to promote high standards in kindergarten work and training classes, because she could praise or criticize as she saw fit. Although the journal included articles designed to educate the reader about Froebelian principles, it mainly reported on all the kindergarten activities brought to Peabody's attention, thereby giving scattered kindergarten pioneers a sense of community. Unfortunately, subscription income did not keep pace with the publishing costs, and in 1875, after two years, Peabody had to cease publication of the journal.

Peabody continued to write and had a regular section in the *New England Journal of Education*. Here a serious controversy arose, however, over two matters: Peabody's criticism of an exhibit labeled "the American Kindergarten" which Anna Coe conducted at the 1876 Philadelphia Centennial Exposition and of Louise Pollock's kindergarten training school which the editor of the *Journal* recommended. Pollock had advertised her training school at the Philadelphia Exposition, claiming to have invented and to have utilized new and different methods and techniques. An even more blatant misuse of the name kindergarten in Peabody's eyes was the Coe exhibit, which encouraged such activities as teaching reading and writing to her class. Peabody objected to their being falsely advertised as kindergarten methods. The purpose of the kindergarten exhibits at the Philadelphia Centennial Exposition, as at other large fairs, was to introduce and demonstrate to visitors from all over the country the idea of the kindergarten; and at this pioneer stage, Peabody argued in favor of not dissipating Froebel's ideas. Although many people defended Pollock and Coe, citing the need to Americanize the kindergarten idea, Peabody maintained that

9

Froebel's system was not the German method but "the human method." At strong odds with the editor of the *Journal* over this matter, Peabody resigned her position on the staff. The *Journal's* editorial staff then published a series of anonymous letters of accusation against her. One letter, signed "Kindergartner," criticized Peabody for treating Froebel "as if he were Christ, his system as . . . a religion, and therefore incapable of improvement, and his pupils as . . . its infallible saints." Another, signed "Justice," railed at Peabody's failure to list Pollock as a reliable training school teacher, calling Peabody unqualified to judge. Elizabeth Peabody never forgave the fact that the accusations were published after her resignation and that she thus had no opportunity to answer her unnamed critics in print.[17]

Peabody then focused her attention on forming a Froebel Society in Boston, with the assistance of five other women from the Boston-Cambridge area, including Louis Agassiz's widow Elizabeth and daughter Pauline Shaw. Modelling their organization on the London Froebel Society, they declared their main purpose to be to raise the quality of kindergarten training. To this end they revived the *Kindergarten Messenger*, establishing it as the Society's publication, and provided scholarships for those talented, promising young women unable to afford proper training. Peabody also hoped that the Society might be able to influence publishers to print books on kindergartening, which she said publishers were loathe to do because they did not find educational books financially lucrative. People read for entertainment, they claimed, not for edification.[18]

A few years later, this Boston group became founding members of a new national association, the American Froebel Union, which Peabody also helped to organize. Baroness Marenholtz had been urging her to create a national society for many years, but she had resisted the suggestion until she thought that a sufficient number of people really understood Froebel's philosophy. A rather prominent group, the original members of the American Froebel Union included people like Henry Barnard, United States Commissioner of Education and editor of the *American Journal of Education*, and William N. Hailmann, director of German-American academies in Louisville and Milwaukee and author of several books translating and explaining Froebel's theory and practice. The organization had goals similar to those of the Boston Society. They too used the *Kindergarten Messenger* as their house organ and provided scholarships for qualified young women seeking training. One of the columns in the *Messenger* recommended the names of those graduates of kindergarten training classes taught by those best qualified to teach them, such as Matilda Kriege, Maria Kraus-Boelte, and Emma Marwedel, all of whom offered solid courses in Froebelian theory and practice.[19]

Peabody often pointed out that the members of the American Froebel Union did not conceive of their functions in negative terms. They did not criticize unqualified teachers, but instead endorsed and lent moral support to the most competent ones. In one instance, for example, Peabody refused to write a derogatory article in the *Kindergarten Messenger* about Anna Coe as she had been requested to do by a group of people in Philadelphia. Peabody personally resented what she described as Coe convincing an "ignorant [school] board" in Philadelphia that she should teach her own system of kindergartening in the normal school. However, while she sympathized with those complaining about Coe's training, she refused to involve herself once again in personal invective, not wanting to put herself in an "autocratic position." Ever since the *New England Journal of Education* published anonymous "insulting letters" to her, she preferred to speak with the backing of a society of "well-known names."[20]

Through all her activities, Elizabeth Peabody succeeded either directly or indirectly in involving innumerable people in the kindergarten cause. Attending one of her early lectures out of sheer curiosity, Milton Bradley, the toy manufacturer, found her enthusiasm contagious. He soon agreed to publish Edward Wiebe's *Paradise of Childhood*, the first American treatise on Froebel's system, and began manufacturing kindergarten materials at a time when no other company did so. First released in 1869, the book became a classic, and Bradley reissued it twenty-five years later. Bradley's partners disapproved of his decision to produce kindergarten materials, which for many years proved a financial loss for the company, but Bradley refused to abandon the project and further manifested his interest by experimenting with the idea of a color wheel and standardization of colored paper. In another case, after a lecture by Elizabeth Peabody in 1874 excited a group of local citizens, Samuel Hill of Florence, Massachusetts, offered his own home for use as a free kindergarten, open to all the children in the town, rich, poor, black, and white. The work grew, and within a few years Hill had built a spacious, well-designed school house with enough room for each child to have a small garden.[21]

Peabody did not have as much success in convincing the Boston School Committee and City Council to open public kindergartens as she did in generating interest in private charity classes. In 1867, she led a petition requesting the school committee to establish kindergartens in the Boston school system, but they rejected the proposal. By 1870, when she again formally recalled their attention to the issue, they agreed to open an experimental kindergarten. However, because of lack of funds and interest, it languished and finally closed in 1879.[22] In the interim, Peabody had interested Pauline Agassiz Shaw in opening charity kindergartens. Her father a famed Harvard professor, and her step-mother dynamic and intelligent and in later years a founder and first president of Radcliffe College, Pauline Agassiz grew up in a financially comfortable and intellectually stimulating home. At the age of nineteen she married Quincey Adams Shaw, who amassed such a fortune in copper mining that at the time of his death in 1908 he was considered one of the richest men in New England. Quincey and Pauline used this vast reserve of money to support their numerous pioneering educational and philanthropic undertakings.

Pauline Shaw's kindergarten activity began in 1877 when she financed the opening of two free kindergartens for children in areas surrounding Boston. When the Boston School Committee closed its experimental public kindergarten class in 1879, Pauline Shaw took it over, opened a training class for teachers, and continued to open kindergartens. By 1883, she had established a network of thirty-one free classes which provided such excellent models that in 1887 they were taken into the Boston public school system. Within a few years, her work had become the single most important such endeavor in that city.[23]

For several years, Elizabeth Peabody corresponded with William Torrey Harris, Superintendent of St. Louis Public Schools and later the United States Commissioner of Education. Although she had been initially unsuccessful in starting public kindergartens in Boston, she sent Harris long letters in 1870 and 1871 urging him to introduce kindergartens into the St. Louis Public Schools. He responded at first with excuses about hot weather and the lack of available space and money. To this she replied that there should be no such thing as economy in education, especially when dealing with something as critical as early childhood. If anything, kindergartens were an economy in the long run, she wrote in another letter. Since children were learning things all the time anyway, and not necessarily desirable things, why not teach them what we know to be helpful and do it in the proper environment? She tried appealing to his ego and to his intellect, attempting to convince him of the kindergarten's importance in philosophical terms hoping that as both a scholar and Superintendent of Schools he would realize its significance. But flatter, cajole, explain as she did, Harris did not become an easy convert to the kindergarten movement. Not until 1873 could Elizabeth Peabody report in the *Kindergarten Messenger* that after many years of reflection Harris had decided to add kindergartens to general public instruction in St. Louis, making it the first city to institute this educational innovation.[24]

But Harris's decision was not only a result of Elizabeth Peabody's prodding: the other woman to influence him was Susan Blow. The beautiful, talented daughter of wealthy, cultured, and deeply religious parents, Susan Blow became acquainted with the kindergarten system in 1871 as a young woman touring Europe with her parents. While there, she spent long days visiting kindergarten classes and taking notes. Kindergartening seemed to be the call to action she had sought before her travels, and it promised to satisfy the gnawing "hunger for something which might seem worthwhile." Upon her return to St. Louis, Susan Blow expressed her desire to start a kindergarten. Although her father offered to finance it, she wanted it to be part of the public school system. She approached Harris about setting up an experimental kindergarten and impressed by her enthusiasm and the extent of her knowledge about Froebel, he agreed to provide her with a classroom and one paid assistant.[25]

Before launching this experiment, however, Susan Blow went to New York City to study kindergartening with Maria Boelte. Boelte had learned kindergartening in Germany under the direction of Froebel's widow, who admiringly referred to Maria Boelte as Froebel's "spiritual daughter." She then spent thirteen years conducting a free kindergarten for poor children in London, where her work became well known and attracted frequent visits from people like Charles Dickens. With the encouragement of Elizabeth Peabody, Maria Boelte came to New York City in 1872 to teach a kindergarten at the private Henrietta Haines School. Susan Blow, who became Boelte's first kindergarten trainee in the United States, was im-

13

pressed by her teacher's "enthusiasm tempered by good common sense."[26]

After a year of study and preparation, Susan Blow returned to St. Louis to open her experimental kindergarten at the Des Peres School in September, 1873. Twenty children enrolled the first day and before long, the forty-two available places were filled. Many children had to be turned away before a new kindergarten could be added in December of that year. The following year, 1874, Susan Blow opened a public training school for kindergarten teachers which she insisted upon running herself. In this way she thought she could assure the competence of each kindergarten teacher entering the St. Louis public school system. Although she received requests from Elizabeth Peabody and the Bureau of Education in Washington, D. C., for lengthy descriptions of the St. Louis work, she refused to send more than cursory reports stating the number of children in attendance, etc., her main reason being: "*the more quietly and modestly* we conduct the kindergarten for the present, the more probability will there be of insuring permanent and satisfactory results."[27]

When Susan Blow wrote the first report of the Des Peres undertaking in the *Annual School Board Report of 1874*, she dealt firmly with the arguments of those who opposed introducing kindergartens into all the public schools. Such people had warned that not enough children would enroll to justify the expense, since parents would not regard school as necessary for three- and four-year-olds, and unless reading were taught, they would not send six-year-olds. However, Susan Blow pointed out that the overflow of applicants required the addition of a second kindergarten two months after the first one had opened. Although skeptics had said that regular attendance would be impossible with such young children, Blow reported 95% attendance, a rate far higher than that of the primary grades. To the assertion that physical exercise was harmful to the children, she retorted that the opposite was true, and her work proved the point. Finally she argued that kindergarten children had performed well in primary work despite the fear that they would not be prepared for it.[28]

The St. Louis experiment soon proved a smashing success. While in 1873 there was one kindergarten, one paid assistant, and Susan Blow as volunteer teacher, by 1879 there were fifty-three classes and 131 paid teachers in addition to numerous unpaid but skilled assistants, many of whom were pupils in Blow's kindergarten training classes. The fulfillment of expectation in St. Louis was a crucial factor in the extension of kindergartens nationally, for it allayed the fears and warnings of those who had been against such an innovation. For anyone in doubt, the accomplishments of the kindergartens were measured in terms of low financial expenditure, high attendance rates, and statistical evidence that kindergarten children outperformed other children in the early primary grades. In addition, the training classes provided teachers for kindergartens throughout the country.[29] The excellent quality of Susan Blow's kindergartens and training classes so impressed Elizabeth Peabody that she referred to St. Louis as "the *sun* of our kindergarten system."[30] For more than a decade, St. Louis remained the sole city which had public kindergartens, and in later years people working to establish public kindergartens in other cities would refer to the St. Louis experiment as the model for all others.

Susan Blow repeatedly stated her position that the most important product of the kindergarten was the personal happiness it brought each child. William Harris, on the other hand, viewed the results of the kindergarten in much more pragmatic terms. Unlike Horace Mann before him and John Dewey later, Harris believed that the role of the school was to adjust the child to society, not to create a new social order. Although he liked Froebel's theory for its recognition of the importance of symbolism, he regarded the kindergarten as excellent industrial preparation, teaching the child manual dexterity, good manners, cleanliness, and industry. He thought that kindergartens were not only important for children of the poor, but also for children of the rich. Their upbringing was all too often left to ignorant servants who merely spoiled them instead of educating them.[31]

Harris stated his position so often that Elizabeth Peabody finally wrote to him that she feared he "did not quite get the idea of Froebel's plays—and the spontaneous growth of the Kindergarten." She understood that as Superintendent of Schools his attention was naturally focused on industrial training and the "school side" rather than the "home side" of the kindergarten; but she also knew that as a philosopher he must appreciate the concept of freedom in the development of the religious feelings which she termed "joy." Peabody valued the kindergarten for *all* children, for its moral and religious influences as well as for its intellectual and scientific foundations. Froebel's theory of education sought to open a child's mind rather than to fill it, and in the process it considered individual differences and a child's creative impulses.[32]

While Harris and Peabody both recognized the significance of environment as well as heredity in man's development, and both felt that preschool children were too often left without needed direction, Harris's goal was to preserve the status quo of society, while Peabody, like her brother-in-law Horace Mann, foresaw a brighter and happier future. Undoubtedly, they spent countless days arguing the question at the Concord Summer School of Philosophy between 1879 and 1888 when they were both regular participants.

1. Ruth M. Baylor, *Elizabeth Palmer Peabody: Kindergarten Pioneer* (Philadelphia: University of Pennsylvania Press, 1965), 47-48, 51, 123, 163; "Elizabeth Palmer Peabody," *Notable American Women, 1607-1950*, III (Cambridge: Harvard University Press, Belknap Press, 1971), 31-34.

2. Mary T. Ryan, "A Garden Where Children Grow," *Wisconsin Journal of Education*, LXXXVI (November 1953), 6-9; Elizabeth P. Peabody, "Our Reason for Being," *Kindergarten Messenger*, I (May 1873), 1; "Margarethe Meyer Schurz" and "Peabody," *Notable American Women*, III, 242-243 and 31-34.

3. Friedrich Froebel, 1827, "Letter to the Duke of Meiningen," quoted in Emilie Michaelis and H. Keatley Moore, translators, *Autobiography of Friedrich Froebel* (Syracuse: Bardeen Co., 1889), 1-101.

4. Friedrich Froebel, *The Education of Man*, William Hailmann, translator (New York: D. Appleton and Co., 1904), 1-2; Froebel, 1827, "Letter to Duke of Meiningen," quoted in Michaelis, *Autobiography*, 74; Froebel to Von Arnswald, Keilhau, September, 1847, quoted in Heinemann, *Froebel's Letters*.

5. Froebel, "Letter to Duke of Meiningen," Michaelis, *Autobiography*, 53-57; Baroness Marenholtz-Bulow, *Reminiscences of Friedrich Froebel*, Mary Mann, translator (New York: C. T. Dillingham, 1877), 64.

6. Friedrich Froebel, *Education of Man*, quoted in Friedrich Froebel, *Friedrich Froebel*, Irene Lilley, translator (Cambridge: Cambridge University Press, 1967), 83-84.

7. Froebel, *Education of Man*, Hailmann, tr., 56-60.

8. Friedrich Froebel, *Pedagogics of the Kindergarten*, Josephine Jarvis, translator (New York: D. Appleton and Co., 1897), 32-60.

9. *Ibid.*, 240. For a description of plays, see 240-285; Marenholtz, *Reminiscences*, 11.

10. Froebel, "Letter to Duke of Meiningen," Michaelis, *Autobiography*, 71-72.

11. Barop, "Critical Moments in the Froebel Community, 1827," *ibid.*, 129.

12. Marenholtz, *Reminiscences*, 53.

13. William N. Hailmann, "Translator's Preface" in Froebel, *Education of Man*; Denton Snider, *Life of Froebel* (Chicago: Sigma Publishing Co., 1900), 428-436; John Kraus, "The Kindergarten in America," *National Education Association*

Proceedings (1877), 194-195; Marenholtz, *Reminiscences*, 200; Baylor, *Peabody*, 99.

14. Peabody, "Our Reason for Being," *Kindergarten Messenger*, I(May 1873), 1.

15. Elizabeth Peabody to William Torrey Harris, February 5, 1877 [?], William T. Harris Collection, Missouri Historical Society (Hereinafter cited as WTH/MHS); Elizabeth Peabody, *Lectures in the Training School for Kindergartners* (Boston: D.C. Heath and Co., 1897), 4-5, 9-64; Elizabeth Peabody to Miss Whiting, n.d., Peabody Collection, Schlesinger Library, Radcliffe College (Hereinafter cited as PC/RC).

16. Peabody, *Lectures*, 88, 13-16, 1-23; Elizabeth P. Peabody to Isabella Mack, Concord, Massachusetts, January 14, 1870 [?], Elizabeth Peabody Collection, Boston Public Library.

17. Elizabeth P. Peabody to William T. Harris, Cambridge, January 19, 1877, and February 5, 1877, WTH/MHS; *Kindergarten Messenger*, New Series I (January and February 1877), 1-3; Peabody, *Lectures in the Training School for Kindergartners*, 85; *New England Journal of Education*, V (January 11, 1877), 21 and (January 18, 1877), 33; Elizabeth P. Peabody to William T. Harris, April 19, 1880 [?], WTH/MHS.

18. Elizabeth P. Peabody to William T. Harris, January 10, 1876 [1877?] and February, 1878, WTH/MHS.

19. See, for example, *Kindergarten Messenger*, New Series I (January and February 1877), 12-18.

20. Elizabeth P. Peabody to William T. Harris, April 19, 1880 [?], WTH/MHS.

21. Henry Blake, "A Sketch of Milton Bradley," *Kindergarten Magazine*, V (April 1893), 587-593; A.L. Weber, "In Memoriam Milton Bradley," *NEA* (1911), 488-490; "Charity Kindergartens in the United States," *American Journal of Education*, XXX (1880), 847; A.D. Mayo, "The Kindergarten at Florence, Massachusetts," *New England Journal of Education*, V (May 24, 1877), 247; *Kindergarten Messenger*, New Series I (July and August, 1877), 111-113.

22. Elizabeth P. Peabody to William T. Harris, Cambridge, Massachusetts, August 25, 1870, WTH/MHS; *Annual Report of the Boston School Committee, 1877*, 18-22.

23. Edwin P. Seaver, "Discussion," *NEA* (1892), 638-40; Charles W. Eliot, "A Tribute," in International Kindergarten Union, *Pioneers of the Kindergarten in America* (New York: The Century Co., 1924), 100-102; "Pauline Agassiz Shaw," *Dictionary of American Biography*, IX (New York: Scribner's Sons, 1957), 46-47; "Pauline Agassiz Shaw," *Notable American Women*, III, 278-280.

24. Elizabeth P. Peabody to William T. Harris, Cambridge, August 25, 1870; Washington, D.C., March 28, 1871; Cambridge, April 25, 1871; Washington, D.C., June 28, 1871, WTH/MHS; Peabody, "Our Reason for Being," *Kindergarten Messenger*, I (May 1873), 1-6.

25. Susan E. Blow to William T. Harris, Cazenovia, July 9, 1892, WTH/MHS.

26. Anna K. Harvey, "Maria Kraus-Boelte, 1836-1918" in International Kindergarten Union Committee of Nineteen, *Pioneers of the Kindergarten in America*, 75-83; Susan E. Blow to William T. Harris, New York, November 14, 1872, WTH/MHS; "Maria Kraus-Boelte," *Notable American Women*, II, 346-347.

27. Susan Blow to William T. Harris, St. Louis, November 10, 1873, WTH/MHS.

28. Susan Blow, "Report of Des Peres Kindergarten," *Annual Report of St. Louis Public Schools*, 1874, 194-199.

29. *Annual Report of the St. Louis Public Schools*, 1878-1879, 187-224.

30. Elizabeth P. Peabody to William T. Harris, April 19, 1877 [?], WTH/MHS.

31. William T. Harris, "The Kindergarten as a Preparation for the Highest Civilization," *Atlantic Educational Journal*, VII (July-August 1903), 35-36. See also Merle Curti, *Social Ideas of American Educators*, Revised Edition (Paterson, New Jersey: Littlefield, Adams and Co., 1965).

32. Elizabeth P. Peabody to William T. Harris [Summer, 1880 ?], WTH/MHS.

CHAPTER II

THE KINDERGARTEN AS AN AGENT FOR URBAN SOCIAL REFORM

Early efforts to introduce the kindergarten to the American public spread out on several fronts. Some people opened teacher training classes so that new kindergartners would have a proper understanding of the ideas and practices of Froebel's system. Some opened private kindergartens or taught kindergarten in a private school. Others focused on school boards and state legislatures in efforts to include kindergartens in public schools. Another group of people, frustrated at the lack of interest by the public schools, turned to organizing free kindergarten associations to support charity kindergartens for children of the poor. These people hoped that free kindergartens would give the slum child a chance he would not otherwise have to enable him to rise above the disadvantages of poverty and neglect. Advocates of the charity kindergarten idea argued that the child continually learned things before he entered school at the age of seven. He learned vice, crime, intemperance, and despair in the slum; but he learned about social relationships, playing, and self-direction in the kindergarten. Reformers, steeped in environmental optimism, sought to change the urban slum pattern by placing three- to seven-year-olds in a kindergarten for three hours a day and by establishing a working relationship with the parents of those children. In most cases, the charity kindergarten expressed a commitment toward helping those whose lives were immersed in the misery of abject poverty. The free kindergarten associations also served the purpose of familiarizing the public with the ideas of the kindergarten and of stimulating support for them.

Pioneer charity kindergartens in Boston, New York City, and San Francisco provided models for later undertakings. In Boston, Pauline Shaw, who had financed her first charity kindergarten in 1877, continued to expand her work. By 1883, she had opened a training class for kindergartners and a network of thirty-one free kindergartens, almost exclusively comprised of children from poor homes. Middle-class youngsters were placed on a waiting list. These Froebelian preschools were models of organization. The teachers, carefully chosen, had to be well-educated women with professional training and experience in kindergartening. They received high salaries and had small classes. If a class had more than twenty children attending, Pauline Shaw hired a recent graduate of a kindergarten training school to assist. Each beautifully furnished room contained a piano, pictures, tables, chairs, and Froebelian equipment.[1]

In addition to financial support, this benefactress took an active interest in all the programs. Although she provided the kindergartens with two excellent supervisors, Colonel Francis Parker observed that she worked "as conscientiously as any regular supervisor of Boston . . ." and watched "intently for any symptoms of wrong method and mistaken directions."[2] The editors of *The New York Times* enthusiastically endorsed her kindergartens, declaring that "few wealthy persons have made better use of the incomes of a large fortune than Mrs. Shaw of Cambridge, Massachusetts." Pauline Shaw, however, preferred anonymity and shunned publicity and praise throughout her life.[3]

At about the same time, R. Heber Newton, pastor of New York City's Anthon Memorial Episcopal Church and well-known social reformer, advised his congregation and the public at large to establish free kindergartens as a means of carrying on the work of social regeneration. He complained that the state common schools ignored the most formative years in a child's development, from infancy to seven years. Under Newton's prodding, an informal association of women from his congregation collected enough subscriptions to open a free kindergarten in 1877 for the numerous poor children living in the neighborhood of their meeting house. Run by Mary Van Wagenen, who had been recommended to the congregation by Maria Kraus-Boelte, the kindergarten op-

20

erated eight months a year, five days a week from 9:30 a.m. to 1:00 p.m., and welcomed all children, regardless of denomination. True to Froebelian philosophy which opposed teaching by drill and rote, Mary Van Wagenen tried to teach the children the communal responsibilities of helping and loving one another, a feat which Newton declared was "not to be effected by the most eloquent exhortations of Sunday-school teachers or of pastors." Experiences in the kindergarten also exposed the children to the importance of a well-balanced diet and of fresh air and cleanliness for proper health, as well as habits of industry and respect for manual and industrial labor.[4]

Also in Manhattan, the newly formed Ethical Culture Society conducted a free kindergarten as part of its regular social work program. Under the leadership of Felix Adler, a group of socially active persons of varying theological views had organized this religious society in 1878. Their bond of unity was commitment to social service, relegating belief in God to a personal decision. They regarded the Ethical Movement as "an effort to accept the fact of pluralism, a recognition of the many ways in which man has sought to find meaning in life." This attitude toward diversity enabled members to work sympathetically and effectively among the poor and the foreign-born in the city. In the first year of its existence the Ethical Society concentrated its energies on three projects: building a model tenement house; providing visiting nursing service; and establishing a free kindergarten for poor children. They saw the nursing service as remedial charity, aimed at relieving existing suffering. The kindergarten was preventive: they hoped it would avert "future unhappiness and misery by educating skillful, intelligent, and independent working men."[5]

The pioneer kindergarten, from which would evolve the later-to-be-famous educational program of the Ethical Culture Society, opened with eight pupils on January 2, 1878. Community distrust of the Society's intentions and suspicion of ulterior motives hampered the endeavor as the rumor spread that the real purpose of the kindergarten was to kidnap the children. However, as the initial group spread the word about their fun, toys, and hot lunches, the number of children steadily increased. Slowly members of the community began to express deeper interest by personally bringing their children to school and occasionally coming in themselves, looking around and asking questions.

21

By the end of the school year, there were twenty-five graduates from the Ethical Society's free kindergarten. Reluctant to send these children into the overcrowded public schools with their rote teaching, the Society accepted the responsibility for continuing their education, using the most progressive techniques. They proposed:

> to erect the entire educational superstructure on the kindergarten foundation, and while varying methods employed according to the ages of the pupils and the subjects taught, to apply throughout the fundamental rule of 'learning by doing.'[6]

In 1880, they started a first grade class and every subsequent year added a new grade until the school was completed. Made possible by a timely and generous gift from Joseph Seligman, the Model School, known as the Workingman's School and later the Ethical School, established the credo that while its graduates might "remain *working* men and *working* women," they might also be "in the best and noblest sense, working *men* and working *women*." Deluged with applications from Ethical Society families, the school implemented a policy of restricting its enrollment of Society members in order to maintain its philanthropic function.[7]

The Ethical Culture Society influenced the formation of kindergartens in California as well as in New York. As a direct result of lectures on education and social reform which Felix Adler delivered in San Francisco in 1878, a group of well-to-do citizens, helped by Adler, organized the Silver Street Kindergarten in the slum area known as Tar Flat. One of the leading figures in establishing this new kindergarten was Emma Marwedel, a Froebel-trained German kindergartner who had been persuaded to come to the United States by Elizabeth Peabody. In 1877 she had directed a small kindergarten training class in Los Angeles, and a year later she invited the outstanding graduate of that class, Kate Smith, to direct the new Silver Street Kindergarten.

Although some of Marwedel's training class pupils had had trouble acclimating themselves to her poor English and impractical nature, Kate Smith had always found her enthusiastic, wise and inspiring:

> Her feet never trod the solid earth; she was an idealist, a dreamer and a visionary, but life is so apt to be crammed with gradgrinds that I am thankful when I come into intimate contact with a dreamer.[8]

Under Marwedel's tutelage, Kate said that she learned that a teacher could create a sense of brotherhood and community in the classroom that, in time, might expand, making "a brotherly world . . . a human possibility." After completing her training and teaching at a private kindergarten for a year, she longed, as she later recalled, "to plant a child-garden in some dreary, poverty-stricken place in a large city, a place swarming with unmothered, undefended, undernourished child life." Kate Smith, who was later to achieve fame as the author of *Rebecca of Sunnybrook Farm* under her married name, Wiggin, eagerly accepted the Silver Street challenge, hoping that "a good many roses might bloom in the desert."[9]

Kate Smith created a kindergarten room that was as beautiful as possible in order to surround the children with an aesthetic environment which she felt they lacked in the "crowded, untidy, noisy, ugly neighborhoods, with their squabbles and fights, their foul smells, their rudeness and vulgarity." The children fulfilled her expectations by responding positively to the beauty, music, and gentleness with which she surrounded them. She observed that they responded to her by not shouting when she spoke to them gently or by becoming aware of their dirty hands when working with delicate pieces of paper. She never felt it necessary to force children to be clean and courteous, for her own experience taught her that they responded that way naturally.[10] A newspaper account of the Silver Street Kindergarten also emphasized the behavioral transformation of many of the children from unruly, aggressive terrors into cooperative, happy children.[11]

The Silver Street Kindergarten, in turn, inspired the opening of other charity kindergartens in San Francisco. Among the numerous visitors to the kindergarten was Sarah Cooper, who conducted a well-attended adult Bible class connected with the Calvary Presbyterian Church in San Francisco. Cooper made her visit during the kindergarten's first year of existence and left convinced that she had found an ideal way to care for poor, neglected children and to provide them with instruction which would emphasize character development. After hearing Sarah Cooper's description of her visit and moved by the desire to put Christianity into action, the Bible class decided to support a free kindergarten at 116 Jackson Street in the heart of the crime-laden Barbary Coast area. Filled with inspiration similar to Kate Smith's, they hoped to brighten the lives of waifs who were left to themselves to roam the alleys by parents too busy, too depressed, or perhaps often too drunk to do otherwise.[12]

23

Under the dynamic leadership of Sarah Cooper and with generous donations, the work of the Jackson Street organization expanded rapidly. Cooper recruited the assistance of the leading newspapers of the city in publicizing her project. A series of articles explained the value of kindergartens in terms of crime prevention, industrial preparation, character building, and a good general "investment for the commonwealth." The simple statement of purpose, which the group used to elicit financial support, appealed to people who were concerned with prevention of crime. With adequate financial support, Cooper secured a capable kindergartner trained by Emma Marwedel and furnished the room with Froebelian equipment, either custom-made or purchased in St. Louis. In order to find pupils for the kindergartens, several of the ladies from the Bible class took to the streets in search of the neediest little children, followed them home, and told the children and their parents about the class. As in the case of the Ethical Society, the Jackson Street Free Kindergarten Association found that visits to the kindergarten disproved community skepticism, and that the parents welcomed the care and training their children received. Even alcoholic mothers, they discovered, often had "enough of real motherhood left to wish to save their hapless ones from a fate so sad as their own."[13]

By the end of the first year, the Jackson Street Kindergarten Association was operating two kindergartens with a total enrollment of 109 children. Ten years later, in 1889, under the new name of the Golden Gate Kindergarten Association, nineteen classes enrolled 1,517 children, and these figures were to double in the following six years. It was about this time that Sarah Cooper referred to the work as a "Public School system on a small scale," and several years later Susan Blow described it as the "largest, wealthiest, best organized and most flourishing association for the extension of the Froebel system."[14]

One of the reasons for this association's financial support was Cooper's ability to solicit funds. Having been a classmate of Leland Stanford in her youth at Cazenovia Seminary, she called on her old friend and enlisted his and his wife Jane's interest and support in her enterprise. Shortly after the tragic death of her son, Jane Stanford donated five thousand dollars, and Sarah Cooper designated the money to be used to start a memorial kindergarten bearing Leland, Jr.'s, name. Moved by that gesture, the mourning mother allocated funds for seven other memorial kindergartens to be organized in the name of her son. Jane Stanford's interest in the kindergartens remained unflagging: she visited them frequently and once even cancelled a trip planned for the following day, deciding to uplift her spirits by attending a kindergarten program. In 1890, she donated a hundred-thousand-dollar permanent endowment to the Association.[15]

Other millionaires contributed to the Golden Gate Kindergarten Association. For example, Mrs. Phoebe A. Hearst donated money for such purposes as the purchase of shoes or annual Thanksgiving and Christmas dinners for the children. She often visited the classes, and one year she and her husband, Senator George Hearst, spent both holidays sharing the festivities with the kindergarten youngsters. In addition, Phoebe Hearst helped found and maintain the Columbia Kindergarten Association in Washington, D.C., serving as its first president in 1893, and she constructed a training school for kindergarten teachers there in 1897. In Anaconda, Montana, and Lead City, South Dakota, where her husband had business interests, she arranged for free kindergartens. On her travels at home or abroad she often took time to seek out and confer with prominent educational figures.[16]

By 1890, Sarah Cooper reported that at various times she had had fourteen millionaires on her Board of Directors. She accounted for such generosity as "the result of perfect consecration to the cause with no possible selfish end in view. God and the angels have inclined human hearts very tenderly toward the children."[17] No doubt her millionaire donors enjoyed hearing such praise.

Sarah Cooper's ability to interest the financial support of smaller businessmen provided still another source of money for the Association. In 1883, the San Francisco Produce Exchange collected a seventy-dollar contribution from its members who wanted to assist in "rescuing from poverty and vice some of the 'grains of humanity,' " and the following year they supported the opening of the Produce Exchange Free Kindergarten. In addition, merchants in one of San Francisco's poorest areas found that the neighborhood had improved in a few short years. Attributing the results to kindergartens in that area, they became voluntary subscribers. Several years later, separate organizations representing merchants, insurance men, realtors and attorneys joined the Produce Exchange, and each one pledged funds to support the opening of a new free kindergarten. Other businessmen offered donations in the forms of goods and services:

for many years Adolph Sutro provided each child in every kindergarten with a tree to plant on Arbor Day; street cars allowed the children to ride free of charge to fairs, parks, and other outings; the Wells Fargo and Company's Express delivered all packages, such as fruits and candies, promptly and free; many offered free clothing; and the President of the Spring Valley Water Company gave free water to all the kindergartens.[18]

Most of all, the Golden Gate Kindergarten Association owed its success to the vigorous direction of Sarah Cooper, whose leadership abilities and religious and social service commitments began in her youth and continued throughout her life. Born Sarah Ingersoll in 1835 in Cazenovia, New York, she began teaching at a district school in a neighborhood village at the age of fourteen. With no church in the community, Sarah took it upon herself to open a Sunday School Bible class for children and adults. In 1852, she was graduated from the Cazenovia Seminary, where her classmates included Philip Armour and Leland Stanford, and then she studied at Miss Willard's Troy Female Seminary. She became a governess in the home of a prominent family in Augusta, Georgia, where she met and married Halsey F. Cooper, the editor and owner of a leading Chattanooga, Tennessee, newspaper. When the Civil War erupted, the Coopers returned to New York State. In 1863, they went back to Tennessee when Halsey was appointed assessor of internal revenue in Memphis. There Sarah Cooper taught a large Bible class for Union soldiers and served as president of the Society for the Protection of Refugees. As a result of her waning health, however, her husband resigned his post and the family moved to California, settling in San Francisco. Regaining her health and with Halsey's encouragement, Sarah renewed her religious and philanthropic activities by teaching a Bible class attended by people of all denominations. The Jackson Street Kindergarten and its successor, the Golden Gate Kindergarten Association, grew out of the work of this class. In addition to these activities, Sarah Cooper belonged to the Pacific Coast Woman's Press Association, Associated Charities of San Francisco, The Century Club, the International Kindergarten Union, and the Pan Republic Congress, where she was one of only five women invited to membership.[19]

For Sarah Cooper, kindergarten work represented an obligation to serve both God and humanity. At one point in her career, she declined an offer of a lucrative position from an insurance company, explaining the decision as follows in a letter to her sister: "I have dedicated my life to God at a very early age—and I have tried to be faithful to that pledge." Although neither she nor any member of the board of her kindergarten association ever received a salary for their services, they, especially their leader and her daughter, worked relentlessly.[20] Sarah Cooper described her typical day this way:

> I rise at 4—I write till ten or eleven—sometimes till noon. I then visit the Kindergartens. Just think of forty teachers—the Matrons—buildings, landlords, and every detail. Then about sixty ladies on the Board. It takes *tact* to keep things running smoothly. But we never have any trouble. But eternal vigilance is the price of success.[21]

Despite the fatiguing pace, her inspiration never seemed to fade. In 1889, she wrote her sister: "Over *6000* little neglected children have been taken from the street by my work and trained for good lives. It is the *great* work of the Age, darling Hattie."[22]

Although Cooper's work began at the Calvary Presbyterian Church, it immediately ran into opposition there. From the start James Roberts, a deacon and a Ruling Elder, disapproved of the idea. Sarah Cooper advised him to go and see the fine work being accomplished in Kate Smith's Silver Street Kindergarten in order to understand what they wanted to do. Visit he did, and Kate Smith recalled his disappointment at discovering that she did not teach specific religious doctrine, but rather that, due to the age of the children and their diverse nationalities and religions, she sought only to surround "the children with enobling influences."[23] A few years later, in 1881, when the Bible class ran a raffle to raise money for the kindergarten, Roberts bitterly chastised Cooper. He reminded her of his visit to the Silver Street class, which he found "supported almost wholly by infidels."

> Your praise of the 'Christian' teacher, and the 'Christian work' that was being done in that school, did not make the school any better in my sight, nor did it raise my estimation of you as an *orthodox, safe teacher* of a Bible Class.[24]

Cooper responded immediately by asserting that the children were "taught the fundamental principles of Christianity—as much as little 3-4 year olds can understand—every day." They learned courtesy, kindness, and respect for others which she hoped would "remain a life-long heritage." The deacon persisted in his antipathy which cul-

27

minated in a heresy trial in 1885. During this period, press coverage was broad and sympathetic to Sarah Cooper. She received many comforting letters, like the one from the Reverend R. Heber Newton in New York City, who pointed to the tragedy of her subjection to gross intolerance when she had performed such inspiring, far-reaching work.[25] Although acquitted in the end, Sarah Cooper chose to leave that Presbyterian congregation and moved her Bible class to a Congregational sponsorship.

During this controversy, Cooper's activities continued unabated, including the publishing of the annual reports of the Jackson Street, later the Golden Gate, Kindergarten Association. Writing them with only the help of her daughter, she used the reports as an educational vehicle to explain the idea of the kindergarten and drum up support for her cause.*

With the dissemination of these annual reports, the Golden Gate Kindergarten Association served as a model for such organizations near and far. Sarah Cooper received voluminous correspondence from all over the world, often requesting either advice on founding a kindergarten association or asking for more copies of her reports. The secretary of the Charity Organization of Buffalo, having found the third annual report an extremely valuable tract, asked for five or six more copies, saying that he hoped his organization's kindergarten work would be as successful as that of the Golden Gate Association. An officer of the New England Publishing Company in Boston wrote to explain that armed with one of Cooper's reports, his daughter had helped to introduce kindergartens in Western Turkey. A Methodist missionary in Chilliwhack, British Columbia, wanted information to help him start kindergartens in his school for Indian children. In 1883, a lady wrote from Dublin, Ireland, that she hoped establishing free kindergartens there might reduce the high crime rate in that city. She pressed the matter for two years in Dublin, continually asking for more reports to distribute, and finally she reported that they had set up classes based on both the reports and Sarah Cooper's personal suggestions.[26]

---

* Since she frequently asked her sister Harriet, apparently her confidante, to read critical portions of annual reports for an opinion on how her work had progressed, it would seem that Cooper refrained from excessive exaggeration to "pad" the reports, despite the fact that she wrote them primarily for publicity and propaganda purposes. See, for example, Sarah Cooper to Harriet Skilton, San Francisco, Calif., January 10, 1888 (HS/CU).

Every year Sarah Cooper sent several reports to Elizabeth Peabody, who distributed them to her friends at home and abroad. One copy reached the chairman of a Women's Christian Temperance Union convention in Texas and resulted in twenty-six W.C.T.U. groups in four states requesting further reports. Still another reached a friend of Elizabeth Peabody in Halifax, Nova Scotia, Cathleen Condon, who wrote that after receiving the Golden Gate's annual reports, she had helped organize a group called "Froebel Institute of Nova Scotia" to spread Froebel's ideas. They hoped ultimately to make kindergartens part of the public schools in that province. She asked for more reports and subsequently wrote again, keeping Cooper informed of their progress.[27]

In addition to the financial support and the increasing interest among many people, the charity kindergarten movement generally was internally successful because of the efforts of the kindergarten teachers to win the respect and cooperation of the community. To effect a closer tie between the kindergarten and the home, almost all of the early free kindergarten teachers spent their afternoons visiting their pupils' families. They tried to explain to mothers what the children did in the classes and to tactfully teach the parents about nutrition, hygiene, and child rearing. When opening her class on Silver Street, Kate Smith recognized the importance of rooting her kindergarten in neighborhood life and kept in constant touch with the parents of her fifty children. She tried desperately to make those parents her allies in caring for the children, and gradually she felt that she had succeeded in growing closer to many of them. She said that in many cases both children and adults appreciated her visits, because many parents, once armed with the knowledge of better ways of discipline, ceased screaming at and beating their children.[28]

The charity kindergartners provided other social services as well to the children and their families. They contacted appropriate organizations, such as the Catholic Aid Society and the Salvation Army, to help the needy. They gave the children warm lunches and provided clothing for many. On one occasion, kindergartners in San Francisco even collected enough money to pay the rent for an impoverished, sickly family about to be evicted from their tenement. Thus, genuine respect and compassion for the children often extended to the families as well. When the 1890's brought hard times financially, Sarah Cooper wrote to her sister that ". . . my sympathies are very largely with the toilers and the strugglers. I hope they will win. Capital is getting too hard on the laboring classes. God help them!"[29]

Kindergartners in San Francisco reported that parents appreciated the opportunities and kindness extended to their children and themselves. Although the illiteracy in English of many adults prevented them from expressing their gratitude in writing, one father sent the following note:

> Many thanks for the Kindness shown to my son, Chester, in giving him a pair of shoes. The year has been a hard one with me, and I appreciate your present highly.[30]

While residents in the vicinity of Silver Street initially greeted Kate Smith with skepticism and wariness, within a short time, she recalled, they shouted cheerful greetings to the approaching "leader of the kid's guards" as they called her, using a corruption of the German term. Evidence also pointed to an increasing self-respect among the adults as parents. The Reverend Mr. Newton told a meeting of the American Froebel Union that in his home visits in his parish, he could tell in which home there had been kindergarten training. A kindergarten child would bring home his work and the mother, although overworked and tired, would decorate the walls. She would clean the windows so that she could hang his work and the design would show through. Also, he found that often the father would stay home in the evenings telling stories to his child and watching him play.[31]

The kindergartens supported by the Anthon Memorial Church and the Ethical Society in New York City, the network of them in Boston, the Silver Street Kindergarten, and the Golden Gate Kindergarten Association represent some of the most influential and exciting pioneer endeavors. All the leading persons in these ventures, the Reverend R. Heber Newton, Pauline Shaw, Felix Adler, Kate Smith Wiggin, and Sarah B. Cooper, were middle to upperclass Americans who viewed with consternation the appalling conditions of the slum districts of their cities. Feeling a moral or religious responsibility, each one turned to the kindergarten as a possible remedy for the brutalizing effects of poverty on children. The idea of preschool education seemed most crucial to them for those children whose parents could not provide them with the type of attention and learning experiences needed to improve their lives. In the years before social settlements, while other organizations were working to help adults, the kindergarten pioneers saw child-saving as the most effective grassroots remedy for the hopelessness and misery in the slums. As the problems of poverty, immigration, and industrialization began to assume alarming proportions during the next two decades, the movement to establish free kindergartens bourgeoned. While there were also numerous tuition-charging kindergartens opened in these years either by individuals or by private schools,[32] the thrust behind the movement to popularize and extend Froebel's ideas for the most part came from philanthropic sources in cities across the country.

1. Elizabeth P. Peabody to William T. Harris, Concord, Massachusetts, December 1, 1880, William T. Harris Collection, Missouri Historical Society.

2. Francis W. Parker, "Boston Kindergartens," *The Kindergarten*, I (March 1889), 335.

3. *New York Times*, December 6, 1878, 4:6; Elizabeth Peabody to Mrs. Lothrop, n.d., Elizabeth Peabody Collection, Schlesinger Library, Radcliffe College.

4. The Reverend R. Heber Newton, "The Free Kindergarten in Church Work," *American Journal of Education*, XXXI (1881), 705-730, 772; a published letter from the Reverend R. Heber Newton, New York City, 1887, to the *Kindergarten Messenger*, I, New Series (May and June 1877), 74-75.

5. Felix Adler, "A Statement of the Aim of the Ethical Culture Society," *Ethical Pamphlet No. 6* (1904), 1-5; Algernon Black, *The Meaning of Ethical Culture* (American Ethical Union, 1960), n.p.; Felix Adler "Report of the District Nursing Department," *United Relief Works of the Society for Ethical Culture, 1881*, 61.

6. Howard B. Radest, *Toward Common Ground* (New York: Ungar Press, 1969), 42-43.

7. "Principal's Report: The Free Kindergarten," *Ethical Society Report, 1881*, 10; Felix Adler, "The Workingman's School," *United Relief Works of the Society for Ethical Culture, 1891*, 15; Director's Report, *Ethical Society Report, 1891*, 19-21, 37-39; *Ethical Culture School Catalog, 1895*.

8. Kate Douglas Wiggin, *My Garden of Memory: An Autobiography* (Boston: Houghton Mifflin Co., 1923), 96.

9. *Ibid.*, 98, 106-107, 110; *Annual Report of the Pioneer Kindergarten Society of San Francisco, 1914*, 7-10.

10. *My Garden of Memory*, 110.

11. *San Francisco Herald*, July, 1880, reprinted in *American Journal of Education*, XXX (1880), 900-902.

12. *First Annual Report of the Jackson Street Free Kindergarten Association, 1879*, 5-7.

13. *Fourth Annual Report of the Jackson Street Free Kindergarten Association, 1883*, 10-11; *First Annual Report of the Jackson Street Free Kindergarten Association, 1879*, 8, 11-12.

14. *Sixteenth Annual Report of the Golden Gate Kindergarten Association, 1895*, 20 (Hereinafter cited as G.G.K.A.); Sarah Cooper to Harriet Skilton, San Francisco, July 21, 1890, and October 25, 1893, Harriet Skilton Papers, Collection of Regional History and University Archives, Cornell University (Hereinafter cited as HS/CU); Susan E. Blow, "The History of the Kindergarten in the United States," *Outlook*, LV (April 1897), 936.

15. Sarah Cooper, "Women in Education: Their Work in the Kindergarten Department," Reprint, 8, Sarah Cooper Papers, Collection of Regional History and University Archives, Cornell University (Hereinafter cited as SC/CU); Jane L. Stanford to Sarah Cooper, September 21, 1885, and November 18, 1886, SC/CU; Sarah Cooper to Harriet Skilton, San Francisco, December, 1890, HS/CU.

16. Phoebe A. Hearst to Sarah Cooper, January 31, 1890, SC/CU; Phoebe A. Hearst to Sarah Cooper, Paris, November 8, 1892, SC/CU; *Twelfth Annual Report of the G.G.K.A., 1891*, 57-58; Phoebe A. Hearst to Sarah Cooper, reprinted in the *Tenth Annual Report of the G.G.K.A., 1889*, 44.

17. Sarah Cooper to Harriet Skilton, San Francisco, July 21, 1890, HS/CU; Sarah Cooper to Harriet Skilton, San Francisco, 1892, HS/CU.

18. John Wightman, Jr., to Sarah Cooper, San Francisco, July 17, 1883, SC/CU; *Twelfth Annual Report of the G.G.K.A., 1891*, 74-75; Sarah Cooper, "The San Francisco Kindergartens," *The California Teacher*, II (March 1884), 505-506; Adolph Sutro to Sarah Cooper, San Francisco, September 22, 1886, SC/CU; *Eighth Annual Report of the G.G.K.A., 1886*, 61.

19. *The Kindergarten News*, II (August-September 1892), 1; a biographical sketch written most likely by her sister, Harriet Skilton, SC/CU; "Sarah Brown Ingersoll Cooper," *Notable American Women, 1607-1950*, I (Cambridge: Harvard University Press, Belknap Press, 1971), 380-382.

20. Sarah Cooper to Hattie Skilton, San Francisco, July 12, 1881, SC/CU; Sarah Cooper to Harriet Skilton, San Francisco, November 17, 1895, HS/CU; *Tenth Annual Report of the G.G.K.A., 1889*, 13.

21. Sarah Cooper to Harriet Skilton, San Francisco, August 7, 1890, HS/CU.

22. Sarah Cooper to Harriet Skilton, San Francisco, December 9, 1890, HS/CU.

23. Wiggin, *My Garden of Memory*, 128-129.

24. James B. Roberts to Sarah Cooper, June 29, 1881, 6-7, SC/CU.

25. Sarah Cooper to James B. Roberts, June 30, 1881, her own copy of the letter sent, SC/CU; The Reverend R. Heber Newton to Sarah Cooper, Garden City, Long Island, December 2, 1885, SC/CU; M. W. Shinn, "Charities for Children in San Francisco," *The Overland Monthly*, Second Series, XV (January 1890), 93-98.

26. Nathaniel S. Roseneau to Sarah Cooper, Buffalo, June 26, 1885, SC/CU; Hiram Orcutt to Sarah Cooper, Boston, May 23, 1890, SC/CU; *Tenth Annual Report of the G.G.K.A., 1889*, 32-34; C. M. Late to Sarah Cooper, Chilliwhack, British Columbia, February 15, 1889, SC/CU; Mrs. Wigham to Sarah Cooper, Killeny County, Dublin, Ireland, March 3, 1883, and June 22, 1885, SC/CU.

27 *Eighth Annual Report of the G.G.K.A., 1887*, 75; Cathleen M. Condon to Sarah Cooper, Halifax, Nova Scotia, February 2, 1888, and April 3, 1888, SC/CU.

28. Wiggin, *My Garden of Memory*, 111-119.

29. *Sixteenth Annual Report of the G.G.K.A., 1895*, 11; Sarah Cooper to Harriet Skilton, San Francisco, July 6, 1894, and July 15, 1894, HS/CU.

30. *Sixteenth Annual Report of the G.G.K.A., 1895*, 112.

31. Lucy Wheelock, "Miss Peabody as I Knew Her," International Kindergarten Union, *Pioneers of the Kindergarten in America* (New York: The Century Co., 1924), 28-29; Wiggin, *My Garden of Memory*, 118.

32. See Laura Fisher, "The Kindergarten," *Report of the United States Commissioner of Education*, I (1903), 690-691 for a description.

CHAPTER III

THE CHARITY KINDERGARTEN MOVEMENT: ATTITUDES AND DEVELOPMENT

During the 1880's, new enthusiasts for the kindergarten movement joined the earlier pioneers in efforts to publicize the significance of establishing more free kindergartens. In their attempts to mitigate some of the common fears of the time and to spark public interest in their cause, these kindergartners stressed those arguments which appealed to traditional America. Their public posture, frequently mixed with class-consciousness, often cast the slum family in a demeaned position and the kindergartner in a patronizing attitude toward her clients. Sometimes, too, they made claims for the movement which were unrealistic, like saying that charity kindergartens would prevent crime. Upon closer examination, much of the rhetoric appeared to consist of arguments that would make a strong impact in an era when people were concerned with the moral, social, and political aspects of good citizenship. This kind of promotional material often failed to emphasize the fact that beneath the superficial aspects of such kindergartners' statements lay a genuine respect for and belief in the dignity of their clients. Certainly these kindergartners reflected their dedication as they moved in and out of children's homes, becoming welcome visitors. In the process of living these beliefs, kindergartners frequently won the cooperation of parents and the community at large, as well as the emulation of other reform organizations which extended kindergartens into social settlement houses and missions.

34

Towards the end of the nineteenth century, as Froebel's philosophy was being implemented by the kindergartners, acceleration of urban growth in the United States made social reform measures increasingly necessary. As the pace of immigration, urbanization, and industrialization quickened and the problems of slums, poverty, and crime intensified, many middle- and upper-class Americans sought to make some kind of ameliorative contribution to the urban predicament. The sudden rise in populations brought about crammed, unsanitary tenement house conditions which were repulsive to genteel, middle-class people. Rapid industrialization, along with the new unlimited labor pool, brought not only low wages but sweat shops, child labor, and long hours which threatened to break down the family structure. Crime appeared to be an inevitable concomitant of these forces, and it was in this direction that kindergartners often focused their attention.[1]

Kindergartners and their supporters frequently spoke of charity preschool classes in terms of arresting crime in its germinal state. For example, in one of his reports as the United States Commissioner of Education, William T. Harris advocated kindergartens because:

> It would be in the interest of good government and of economy to get hold of these persons and properly care for them before germs of evil are planted in their susceptible young lives.[2]

Crime, said Sarah Cooper, could not be prevented by punishment but by starting at an early age to prepare children "for useful and honorable citizenship," and to this ultimate end the kindergarten should train the children in the virtues of honesty and self-control. Kindergartner Angeline Brooks agreed that the kindergarten had no rival as a preventive of crime, and many organizations, such as the Brooklyn Free Kindergarten Association, appealed to donors and supporters on this basis. They argued that considering the number of neglected children and the increasing number of them who went "to the bad" before the age of seven, it was shortsighted to ignore children at the age when they could be saved from evil ways.[3]

Many kindergartners believed that if they indoctrinated a belief in God and moral social behavior in their students, they would be teaching them the concepts of good citizenship and in doing so they would prevent crime. For example, with characteristic optimism, one writer explained that since "every human vice is a perverted virtue," the kindergartner needed only to cultivate the virtue to stamp out the vice. Another summed up the kindergarten as a community in which the underprivileged child found his "soul power."[4] Sarah Cooper hoped that using the Ten Commandments and the Golden Rule as the basis for inculcating proper behavior would in turn bring out the spiritual nature of the child.

> It is the aim of the kindergarten to lead the little ones to their Heavenly Friend. They are taught to love Him. They are taught to love one another, to help one another, to be kind to one another, to care for one another. No one can love God who does not love his fellows.[5]

Amalie Hofer, editor of *The Kindergarten Magazine*, regarded a belief in God as an essential prerequisite for anyone who wanted to become a kindergartner. Approaching religion from a broader perspective, Elizabeth Harrison said that kindergartners needed to teach the children about "the common brotherhood of all mankind," because, "we cannot say with truth, 'Our Father who art in Heaven' until we can say our brother who is on earth." In the same spirit, the Chicago Froebel Association chose to emphasize its non-sectarian spirit and explained that it used the Bible in its training classes for teachers and in its free kindergartens only on a symbolic level as a means of helping the children in their daily work and conduct.[6]

Enthusiasts, however, often found themselves making exaggerated claims in terms of crime prevention. The Reverend R. Heber Newton advised that the state would find free kindergartens as a preschool department in the public schools a cheap but worthwhile investment: "What it would spend there it would save in our prisons." Jacob Riis, in *Children of the Poor*, referred to the kindergarten as a "jail deliverer," and Sarah Cooper maintained that public schools did not get to the little waifs who would become criminals early enough nor in the proper manner. She quoted Juvenal, Plato, Aristotle, Bacon, Lycurgus, and others as having emphasized the importance of reaching children in their early years when they were most pliable, so as to develop their virtuous potential and to wipe out the bad. "The design of the kindergarten," she said, "was to prevent crime,"[7] and she often left her audience with the grim reminder that:

> from a single neglected child in a wealthy community in the State of New York there had come a notorious stock of criminals, vagabonds

36

and paupers, imperilling every dollar's worth of property and every individual in the community. Not less than twelve hundred persons have been traced as the lineage of six children who were born of this one perverted and depraved woman, who was once a pure, sweet, dimpled little child, and who, with proper influences thrown about her at a tender age, might have given to the world 1200 progeny who would have blest their day and generation.[8]

Kindergarten associations frequently adopted mottoes for the covers of annual reports reflecting their social or civic concern. The Elm City Free Kindergarten Association in New Haven, Connecticut, quoted Richard Watson Gilder, editor of *Century* magazine:

Plant a free kindergarten in any quarter of a crowded metropolis and you have begun, then and there, the work of making better homes, better citizens and a better city.[9]

Similarly, the motto of the Silver Street Kindergarten Society read:

Education is a better safeguard of liberty than a standing army.[10]

There was, however, precious little specific evidence to back up these claims. The Golden Gate Kindergarten Association reported in 1893 after following the San Francisco police records that only one of the nine thousand slum children who had attended their kindergartens had been later charged with crime. More modest proof came from merchants along Front Street in the same city who reported less mischief, fewer broken windows, and less petty thievery. Also, kindergartners observed that after a short time in their classes, children evidenced more cooperative behavior and a greater pride in their appearance as shown by personal cleanliness and neater attire. The *Sixteenth Annual Report* of the Golden Gate Kindergarten Association boasted having directed the talent of many of its pupils into constructive channels: one young man became the brightest apprentice in a brass foundry, while another, who at the age of four was called "The King Hoodlum of the Barbary Coast," underwent a complete transformation and became a successful lawyer.[11]

Some kindergartners chose to minimize the immediate benefits to society of kindergarten training; rather they preferred to speak of the development of a child's sense of self-control and self-government in terms of the child's own needs, not necessarily those of society. William N. Hailmann, Superintendent of Schools in Mil-

37

waukee, Maria Kraus-Boelte, John Kraus, Kate Douglas Wiggin, her sister, Nora A. Smith, and Susan Blow wrote books probing the issues of child development and how to respond to them in the kindergarten. In her *National Kindergarten Manual*, Louise Pollock emphasized that the true kindergartner did not use force, ridicule, or prizes to get the children to behave in a particular fashion; nor did she regard keeping the children still as a goal or an achievement worthy of merit.[12]

In a lecture before the National Conference on Charities and Corrections, Kate Wiggin criticized glib statements about education as a panacea for reducing the crime rate. She said that it was more meaningful to speak in terms of principles of child development than in terms of crime prevention. She told her audience that the past and present educational systems had not been geared to affect children's behavior constructively. In the kindergarten, however, a child learned self-direction through attempts at rational discipline, as opposed to "blind obedience to arbitrary command." She found this approach worthwhile even if it took more trouble and energy to infuse "the spirit of this kind of discipline into family and school . . ." for, she continued, "life is a good deal of trouble anyway, if you come to that." Kate Wiggin maintained that in the kindergarten the child cultivated practical habits of virtuous everyday living by working and playing cooperatively. A child learned, for example, to take care of her art materials because there were just enough for each pupil. She also learned consideration for others through guidance from the kindergartner who might say, for example: " 'Let us save all the crumbs from our lunch for the birds, children. Do not drop any on the floor: it will only make work for somebody else.' " Thus, Wiggin explained the moral training in the kindergarten not in terms of a series of memorized precepts or recited prayers, but in terms of constant experiences of active choices. She thought that handwork, although popularly and superficially valued for its industrial potential, aimed at developing the child's aesthetic and creative instincts. Despite criticism that too much play was harmful to children, Kate Wiggin contended that happiness and joy contributed to a morally constructive environment for childhood.[13]

With this knowledge of their public positions, we must then assess more closely some of the kindergartners' attitudes toward poverty-stricken or immigrant families and their children. Naturally these attitudes varied, but in general seem to have borne out Lillian Wald's observation that the same person who might label adult immigrants as anarchistic, dirty, and ignorant will melt at the sight of lively, playful children and see his responsibility to them.[14] However, that is not to say that kindergarten literature was not at times filled with patronizing remarks. Descriptions of lower-class children ranged from condescending to sympathetic, frequently tainted with sentimentality. An example of a compassionate reaction to the effects of living conditions of the poor in large cities is depicted in an article in *The Kindergarten*. The most unfortunate victim, the author declared, was invariably the "street waif," sent out in his tender years to beg or earn a few pennies. Froebel, he continued, was surely to be praised for realizing the importance of early childhood education, because there in the kindergarten the "forlorn, neglected little beings" learned to respond to kindness.

> We have seen the lip quiver and the eye fill with tears, when instead of the harsh reproof and the sharp cuff to which he has been accustomed, a hand has been softly laid on the shoulder and kind words have fallen on his ear.[15]

Similarly, a note in the same periodical told of the opening of a charity kindergarten in Baltimore to salvage the lives of "eight forlorn and abject little ones . . . whose faces showed familiarity with degradation and vice."[16]

Other remarks reflected a sense of class-consciousness which marked more acutely the dichotomy between the stratum of society from which the kindergartner came and the one to which she entered. For example, one kindergartner recommended the kindergarten as a cure for "the ignorance and unbridled passions of the lower classes of society." Another kindergartner, Constance Mackenzie, explained that the one thousand children enrolled in the free kindergartens run by the Sub-Primary School Society of Philadelphia came "mostly from the poorest and most ignorant classes, frequently from the most degraded and vicious." A woman involved in free kindergarten work in Chicago described the children as coming "from the lowest of the low," while another kindergartner assured her readers that "the poor and wayward" were "as good as we . . . , but they have through weakness fallen by the wayside." Lack of cleanliness always seemed to bring out

39

intolerance in kindergartners as in one kindergartner's description of immigrant children as "dirty little savages."[17]

Attitudes toward the immigrant poor spanned an even wider spectrum, ranging from the snobbishness noted above to a deep-seated respect for immigrant problems and culture. At one extreme, a teacher in a mission kindergarten in Lackawanna, Pennsylvania, described immigrant parents as ignorant in such a way as to imply that ignorance and the inability to speak English were synonymous. Another writer of a kindergarten association report spoke admiringly of those immigrant parents who called their children by American names like Joseph rather than Italian names like Giusseppe, because she said such parents were more likely to become loyal American citizens. This kindergartner also found the "quaint sayings of the children" and the "disjointed English of the parents" quite amusing, failing to understand their serious efforts to communicate. Often teachers in kindergartens which catered to foreign children ignored any knowledge the child may have had of a second language or the richness of his cultural heritage. Some kindergartners emphasized the need to cultivate manners and refinement and the necessity of laying a foundation for industrial training. They hoped such training would develop the habits of thrift and industry and promote manual dexterity, all of which in turn would discourage pauperism and intemperance.[18]

The same patronizing attitude toward minority cultures is reflected in the testimony of a kindergartner working with American Indian children. Armed with both her concern and her own ideas of cultural superiority, Lucie Maley started her kindergarten classes on the reservation by teaching the children to make teepees and moccasins, but she quickly changed her tack and tried to teach them about the goodness and purity of the white child's home life. When she found that Indian parents did not instill the pride of individual ownership in their children, she tried to remedy the matter by providing each child with a plant that he had to care for by himself, an activity similar in spirit to the Dawes Severalty Act passed by Congress in 1887. Maley believed that although the children had inherited cruel and savage dispositions, she had opened their hearts to the beauty of nature as well as to God, love, discipline, courtesy and patriotism.[19]

On the other hand, many kindergartners spoke of foreigners with understanding and respect. Emma Marwedel, writing of a kindergarten whose children represented French, Spanish, Mexican, Italian, Slav, Austrian, Puerto Rican, Japanese, and Chinese nationalities, used "hard-working" and "thrifty" to describe the parents, except in the case of some Mexicans who, hampered by illness and lack of work, she said, lived in abject poverty. There was no apparent condescension in the reports from teachers at the Ethical Society Kindergarten in New York City. Workers from the Chicago Kindergarten Institute discovered to their pleasure that at the Jewish Settlement most parents personally brought their children to class every day. They found that although the parents could provide their children with very few material possessions, they gave them love and encouragement. Other kindergartners also spoke of parental interest, such as mothers visiting at the doorway. Maud Conliff, for many years the leader of a Presbyterian mission kindergarten in a Bohemian neighborhood in Baltimore, found the families very appreciative of all that was done for their children, always opening their doors to the visits of the kindergartner and taking great pride in listening to all that their youngsters had learned. Conliff's reports also displayed a deep understanding of the daily problems facing the immigrant family living on a tight budget. Another teacher indicated that often native American children who came from homes where parents deprecated immigrants learned greater tolerance from their experiences in a kindergarten of children from mixed ethnic backgrounds.[20]

Although it is difficult to draw an exact line distinguishing honest convictions from rhetorical appeals aimed at securing public support, it does appear that kindergartners exhibited varying degrees of concern with those social problems which agitated society in general, such as vice, intemperance, and sloth. However, in addition to their responsibility to society and the needs of the child, these women saw the boundaries of their duties extended into the home and the community. Home visiting became an integral part of their work. While attempting to explain certain aspects of child development, nutrition, hygiene, and alternative methods of discipline to the parents, kindergartners also learned more about the children attending their classes. The mutual interest of teacher and mother in the child may have facilitated visits, but the kindergartner still had to visit the homes frequently in order to win the complete confidence of the mother. Once that trust and rapport was established the kindergartner often found the mother responsive to her suggestions.[21]

41

Home visiting provided opportunities to influence the quality of home life. The teacher of the charity kindergarten supported by St. George's Episcopal Church in New York City, where George Rainsford was the pastor, found one mother who had given her child paper and glue to play with so that she would not disturb the sick man living below. She also found that the children's songs and games often entertained the whole family. The Elm City Free Kindergartens allowed children to take home their toys, such as books, puzzles, bicycles, and sleds, on a rotating basis. Teachers noted in their home visits that these toys brought pleasure to all members of the family, and although everyone played with them, they rarely returned broken. In a report based upon replies from those engaged in free kindergarten work, Constance Mackenzie said that the kindergartners were certain that the effects of their work were felt in homes in terms of cleanliness, tidiness, gentler speech, and behavior. They even found more attractive decorations in the houses and apartments.[22]

In addition to home visiting, kindergartners attempted to maintain a relationship with the families by holding mothers' meetings which were a derivation of Froebel's idea that mothers must be trained in the ways of child development and in kindergarten techniques. Mothers' meetings took on added meaning in crowded urban centers where harassed women often appreciated the advice, interest, and hints offered by the trained kindergartner. Ignorance of nutrition and child care plagued many a mother. John Spargo in *The Bitter Cry of the Children* (1906) described vividly the mother who fed sausage, bread, and pickles to her seven-week-old infant who died shortly of gastritis. Kindergartners found similar instances, such as a twenty-one-year-old Italian mother of four children who came to the kindergarten to complain that the milk her child drank in that class made the child sick. She served only coffee and wine at home.[23]

In planning their mothers' meeting, kindergartners were advised to visit each home to better understand the environment, but to offer no unsolicited advice, keeping in mind that:

> No matter how sordid and poor the district is in which the kindergarten is placed . . . the privacy and rights of the nearest house should be as sacred to her as any mansion on Capitol Hill

and that:

Cleanliness and order are not always possible when living in two rooms with six children.[24]

Kindergartners were further advised to send home to each mother a written invitation to the meeting; to provide care for the tots who could not be left at home; to serve simple, inexpensive refreshments as cheerfully as possible; and always to have flowers on the table, if only dandelions. Above all, the kindergartners were reminded that mothers were pulled in many directions and their time was precious, and therefore the meetings should be made as interesting and meaningful as possible.

At such meetings, kindergartners explained the purpose and activities of the kindergarten and lectured on practical subjects, or held informal discussions. Lecture topics included the importance of adequate ventilation, child care in sickness and in health, buying and cooking foods, sewing children's clothes, and personal and domestic hygiene. The teachers urged parents, for example, to refrain from physical punishment, to have confidence in their children, and to be as responsible and patient as possible with them. Frequently, kindergartners conducted informal discussions on problems of interest to most mothers, such as discipline, family outings, and children's questions concerning sex. They tried to help the mothers analyze and solve problems, always trying to emphasize the individuality of each child. Sometimes language presented a barrier if only a few of the mothers spoke or understood English, but this was remedied by having someone present at the meeting who spoke both the foreign and the English languages and served as translator.[25]

Generally, kindergartners regarded mothers' meetings as one of the most significant aspects of their duties, realizing the need for parental cooperation if their work was to have any lasting meaning. They found that most mothers eagerly engaged in the child study offered at those sessions. The Silver Street Kindergarten Society even succeeded in 1896 in getting fathers to attend their regular monthly parents' meetings. In Louisville, Kentucky, New York City, and Boston, associations found enthusiastic responses to mothers' clubs where the mothers held offices and planned programs while the kindergartner acted only as an adviser. Many of these clubs continued to have active members whose children were long past kindergarten age. Boston kindergartner Lucy Wheelock found one mother's statement representative of others: "The meetings are the

43

only bright spot in the month—the only time I get something bright to think of."[26]

For the immigrant community itself, then, the importance of the kindergarten lay in its attempts to strengthen family relationships and to narrow the breach between the foreigners and their Americanized children. To this extent, the home visits and mothers' meetings were welcomed by the immigrant parents.

One outgrowth of the kindergartners' involvement with mothers was the start of other associations. The Annual Convocation of Mothers held under the auspices of Elizabeth Harrison's Chicago Kindergarten College became the forerunner of the National Congress of Mothers organized in 1897 by Mrs. Alice Birney. Kindergartners like Elizabeth Harrison and Lucy Wheelock were active in this organization, which later became known as the National Congress of Parents and Teachers, or P. T. A. Reflecting attitudes prevalent among kindergartners, the founders of the National Congress of Mothers felt that rich and poor mothers alike needed to be educated regarding the moral, physical, and mental development of their children. Despite the fact that few poor mothers attended, they regarded:

> Its [the Congress's] province . . . as much in the interest of the puny, neglected, under-exercised children of the rich as in the same class of children of the poor.[27]

In addition to their educational relations with the child and his parents, kindergartners also involved themselves in neighborhood problems. They felt called upon to provide necessary community services essential to the well-being of the families involved. For example, in 1886 when fire ravaged a section of San Francisco, leaving five to six hundred people homeless with only the clothes on their backs, the teachers and assistants at the Stanford Kindergarten opened their large rooms to care for and house the stricken families until more substantial relief could be provided. In most of its kindergartens, the Golden Gate Kindergarten Association hired women to wash, clothe, and furnish a warm breakfast for those youngsters who needed it.[28] Almost all charity kindergartens provided the child with milk and crackers every day, this often being the child's only daily milk. Many also provided a warm lunch.

In appreciating the problems of the immigrant parents and their earnest desire to improve their lives and their children's lives, the

44

mental set of the kindergartner resembled that of the settlement worker. "A social settlement in embryo," is the picture one kindergartner portrayed; the social settlement was the "adult kindergarten," said Amalie Hofer; and "Every Kindergarten a College Settlement" was the title of one section of Sarah Cooper's *Sixteenth Annual Report*.[29]

Indeed, beneath the hyperbole of these statements there lay a close relationship between the two movements. In 1887, when Dr. Stanton Coit opened the Neighborhood Guild, the first social settlement house in the United States, he immediately found two experienced kindergartners to help him start classes for young children. Jane Addams recalled the kindergarten at Hull House as their "first organized undertaking," a pattern followed by successive settlements, like Chicago Commons, New York College Settlement, and Alfred Corning Clark Neighborhood House. Kindergartens represented an excellent opening wedge into the community; at the same time, Froebel's progressive educational principles of developing the whole child appealed to the social values of the settlement workers. Through mothers' clubs and home visiting, kindergartners helped settlement workers become established and accepted in the community. This involvement is explicit in Jane Addams' description of the Hull House Kindergartner who, she said, was filled with "mirth and buoyancy" and whose "eager desire to share the life of the neighborhood never failed, although it was often put to the test." The Elizabeth Peabody kindergarten Settlement House, one of the earliest settlements in Boston, uniquely combined the two movements. In the Peabody House, resident workers were kindergartners and students attending normal schools, and they conducted a kindergarten as their main activity in getting involved in the lives of the children and their community.[30]

The settlement movement gave the kindergarten movement increased impetus: all settlements maintained one or more kindergartens at some time during their existence. Graham Taylor, founder of the Chicago Commons, encouraged the founding of the Chicago Kindergarten Institute to meet the growing demand for properly trained kindergartners, and students of this institution did much of their practice teaching at the kindergartens of the University of Chicago Social Settlement, Chicago Commons, Northwestern University Social Settlement, and others. In addition, kindergartens at settlements played a key part in summer programs for children which

45

usually included a vacation school, playground facilities, and a summer kindergarten held in a rooftop garden to relieve the children's boredom. Many settlements also had a summer house where the preschool children and many of their mothers spent a few weeks. During the year, Kindergarten Graduate Clubs offered programs for school-aged children based on Froebelian principles and activities.[31]

Nothing functions in a vacuum, however, and settlement activities appear to have affected the program of many kindergarten associations. Although kindergartners had long since realized the necessity of extending their work into the community, a renewed emphasis on this aspect of the kindergarten program began in the 1890's and 1900's. In those decades, numerous articles and reports stressed the importance of the kindergarten as a community center for the neighborhood. By 1898, for example, the Indianapolis Free Kindergarten and Children's Aid Society supported thirteen free kindergartens plus domestic training schools, mothers' classes, literature and science clubs for boys and girls, nursery maids' clubs, and social entertainment for the families of each district. In addition to supporting several kindergartens, the Silver Street Society offered Housekeeper's Classes based on Emily Huntington's Kitchen-Garden program for girls aged nine to fifteen and maintained a free library and reading room with a daily average attendance of sixty.[32]

Often, too, kindergarten associations cooperated with settlements in attacking a variety of problems. The New York Association provided meals for many of the undernourished children at the Nurses Settlement, later called the Henry Street Settlement. In Chicago, Mrs. Alice Putnam of the Chicago Froebel Association taught her training class in a newly acquired building at Hull House, thereby helping the residents of that settlement to afford the cost of the new property.[33]

In addition to settlement houses, other organizations, such as missions and the Women's Christian Temperance Union, adopted kindergartens as part of their work. A Presbyterian missionary summed up the advantages of working with the young child this way:

> In the kindergarten, the wee ones are easily led into the English tongue, American ways and Christian influences. As a wedge into the homes and an avenue to the parents' hearts, the kindergarten is indispensable.[34]

46

A Baltimore Quaker spoke of the kindergarten as an inestimable aid in converting families to his faith. The Women's Christian Temperance Union established several of its own kindergartens as part of its preventive work. We have already noted the enthusiastic endorsement of kindergartens by the national W.C.T.U. convention in 1886. Most kindergartners strongly supported temperance. Many even advocated the use of specific temperance lessons in the classroom, such as teaching the child to like tea, to realize the immorality and vulgarity that result from imbibing alcoholic beverages, and to say "no, thank you," to anything but tea, lemonade, milk, soda water, or hot water. One kindergartner suggested the motto: "The drunkard and the glutton shall come to poverty." Writers in the kindergarten journals often chastised kindergartners who did not express strong temperance views.[35]

A kindergartner, then, in her varied duties had to be an exceptionally talented woman, knowing how to deal effectively with the child in relation to the parent, school, and society. In addition to her training in kindergarten principles, she needed tact, understanding, honesty, and gentleness. She was not a classroom babysitter, but actually entered people's homes and attempted to share a part of their lives. She had to prove herself in order to win acceptance in the neighborhood. If she started out with deprecating thoughts, she had to disguise them in order to win the trust and respect of her pupils' parents. Perhaps many poor and immigrant women, intimidated or flattered by the interest, accepted the brashest of kindergartners into their homes, but others were poor but proud and would not have taken kindly to a fancy lady with a snobbish air interfering in their lives. Despite the deep division between many of the kindergartners' social and economic backgrounds and their choice of profession, the wide community acceptance reported indicates that, for the most part, kindergartners learned to evidence a keen respect for their clients. For example, when Elizabeth Harrison first set up kindergarten study clubs in Chicago, they were for "mothers of the educated class." But in 1892, when she started classes in the poorer areas of the city for the mothers of children already attending free kindergartens, she found it a "great revelation" to see "the earnestness and the interest and the loyal intelligence of the class of women ordinarily known as the char-women of the city."[36]

Through her efforts in the classroom and in the homes, the kin-

47

dergartner idealistically hoped to offset the inevitable scars caused young children by the hardships of poverty and to offer new opportunities for a better life. Regarding environment as the more significant aspect in the nature versus nurture controversy, the kindergartner sought to create an atmosphere which would develop the potential of each individual child.

1. For a more detailed understanding of this period, see Lawrence A. Cremin, *The Transformation of the School* (New York: Alfred A. Knopf, Inc., 1961), 1-176; Aaron Abell, *The Urban Impact on American Protestantism: 1865-1900* (Cambridge: Harvard University Press, 1943), 1-26, 164-165; Robert H. Bremner, *From the Depths* (New York: New York University Press, 1964), 31-45; Timothy L. Smith, "Progressivism in American Education: 1880-1900," *Harvard Educational Review*, XXX (Spring, 1961), 168-193; Henry F. May, *The Protestant Churches and Industrial America* (New York: Harper and Bro., 1949), 91-235; Moses Rischin, *The Promised City: New York's Jews: 1870-1914* (Cambridge: Harvard University Press, 1962), 1-18, 51-94, 171-194.

2. *Report of the United States Commissioner of Education, 1892-1893*, 1646.

3. Sarah B. Cooper, "Practical Results of Ten Years' Work," *National Conference on Charities and Corrections Proceedings* (1889), 193 (Hereinafter cited as *NCCC*); Cooper, "The Kindergarten as a Child-Saving Work," *NCCC* (1882), 132-133; Angeline Brooks, "A Mission Kindergarten," *Lend A Hand*, II (July 1887), 415-419; *First Annual Report of the Brooklyn Kindergarten Association, 1891-1892*, 11-12; Stella McCarty, "Charity and the Kindergarten," *The Charities Review*, VII (January 1898), 949.

4. McCarty, "Charity and the Kindergarten," 946-947; "Potpourri," *The Kindergarten*, III (March 1891), 417.

5. Sarah B. Cooper, "The Kindergarten in its Development of Faculty," *The Kindergarten*, I (September 1888), 3.

6. Amalie Hofer, "The Christ in Education," *Kindergarten Magazine*, IV (December 1892), 194-195; Sarah B. Cooper, "The Kindergarten as a Character Builder," *NCCC* (1885), 223-224; Elizabeth Harrison, "Discussion," *National Education Association* (1892), 694 (Hereinafter cited as *NEA*); "The Chicago Free Kindergarten Association," *Kindergarten Magazine*, V (June 1893), 737.

7. The Reverend R. Heber Newton, "The Bearing of the Kindergarten on the Prevention of Crime," *NCCC* (1886), 58; Jacob Riis, *Children of the Poor* (New York: Charles Scribner's Sons, 1892), 181; Sarah B. Cooper, "The Kindergarten in its Bearing Upon Crime, Pauperism, and Insanity," *NCCC* (1893), 89-94.

8. *First Annual Report of the Jackson Street Free Kindergarten Association, 1879*, 11.

9. *Elm City Free Kindergarten Association Report, 1919-1920*, n.p.

10. *Silver Street Kindergarten Society, 1896*, front cover.

11. Sarah B. Cooper, "The Organic Union of Kindergarten and Primary School," *NEA* (1893), 341; *Third Annual Report of the Jackson Street Free Kindergarten Association, 1881*, 6-7; *Sixteenth Annual Report of the Golden Gate Kindergarten Association, 1895*, 170.

12. William N. Hailmann, *Kindergarten Culture in the Family and Kindergarten* (New York: Van Antwerp, Bragg & Co., 1873); Maria Kraus-Boelte and John Kraus, *The Kindergarten Guide* (New York: E. Steiger and Co., 1877); Kate D. Wiggin and Nora A. Smith, *Froebel's Occupations* (Boston: Houghton Mifflin Co., 1897); Susan E. Blow, *Symbolic Education* (New York: D. Appleton & Co., 1894); Louise Pollock, *The National Kindergarten Manual* (Boston: De Wolfe, Fiske, and Co., 1889), 7-10.

13. Kate Douglas Wiggin, "The Relation of the Kindergarten to Social Reform," *NCCC* (1888), 247-258.

14. Lillian Wald, *The House on Henry Street* (New York: Henry Holt and Co., 1915), 66-67.

15. E. J. Jameson, "The City Waif," *The Kindergarten*, III (September 1890), 19-20.

16. "Potpourri," *The Kindergarten*, I (December 1888), 255.

17. Angeline Brooks, "The Theory of Froebel's Kindergarten System," *The Kindergarten and the School* by Four Active Workers (Springfield: Milton Bradley Co., 1886), 48; Constance Mackenzie "Free Kindergartens," *NCCC* (1886), 50; *Report of the U.S. Commissioner of Education, 1882-1883*, cv; "Potpourri," *The Kindergarten*, III (March 1891), 417; "Editorial," *Kindergarten News*, III (May 1893), 111; *Annual Report of the Elm City Free Kindergarten Association, 1919-1920*, n.p.

18. Dora Hansen, "Luzerne Kindergarten," *Home Mission Monthly*, XVIII (May 1904), 154-155; *Annual Report of the Pioneer Kindergarten Society of San Francisco, 1914*, 16-17; *Annual Report of the Elm City Free Kindergarten Association, 1919-1920*, 12-13; Newton, "The Bearing of the Kindergarten on the Prevention of Crime," 56-57; Cooper, "The Kindergarten as a Character Builder," 227-229; "Editorial," *Kindergarten News*, III (May 1893), 111; Eva Magruder, "Self-control in the Kindergarten—Foundation Temperance Work," *Kindergarten Magazine*, III (November 1890), 143-144.

19. Lucie Maley, "Benefit of the Kindergarten to the Indian Children," *Kindergarten Magazine*, X (March 1898), 438-441.

20. Emma Marwedel, "Kindergarten Report," *Pioneer Kindergarten Society of San Francisco Annual Report, 1914*, 23; Laura Whitney, "Christmas in a Jewish Kindergarten," *Kindergarten Magazine*, XVIII (December 1905), 193-198; Hortense Orcutt, "The Kindergarten and the Family of the Little Foreigners," *Kindergarten-Primary Magazine*, XXIII (November 1910), 86-87; "Little Foreigner in Baltimore," *Home Mission Monthly*, XX (August 1906) 251-252; Maud Conliff, "A Bohemian Kindergarten in Baltimore," *Home Mission Monthly*, XXIII (January 1909), 73; Anna G. Spencer, "The Changing Population of Our Large Cities," *Kindergarten-Primary Magazine*, XXIII (November 1910), 65-71; *Report of the Workingman's School, 1884*.

21. Laliah B. Pingree, published letter in *Report of the U.S. Commissioner of Education, 1882-1883*, cvii.

22. *St. George's Yearbook* (1892), 256; *Elm City Free Kindergarten Association Annual Report, 1919-1920*, n.p.; Constance Mackenzie, "Free Kindergartens," *NCCC* (1886), 51. See also Riis, *Children of the Poor*, 174-187; Richard Watson Gilder, "The Kindergarten: An Uplifting Social Influence in the Home and District," *Kindergarten Magazine*, XVI (November 1903), 130.

23. John Spargo, *The Bitter Cry of the Children* (Chicago: Quadrangle Books, 1968), 28; *Elm City Free Kindergarten Association Annual Report, 1919-1920*, n.p.

24. Wilhelmina T. Caldwell, "Mothers Meetings Among the Poor," *The Kindergarten News*, V (October 1895), 283.

25. *Ibid.*, 283-285; Helen L. Duncklee, "The Kindergartner and her Mothers' Meetings," *Kindergarten Review*, X (September 1899), 12-15; *Brooklyn Kindergarten Association Annual Report, 1891-1892*, 14-15; *Elm City Free Kindergarten Association Annual Report, 1919-1920*, n.p.; *Twelfth Annual Report of the Golden Gate Kindergarten Association, 1891*, 20-21; "Reports," *Kindergarten Magazine*, III (November 1890), 160-161; Elizabeth Harrison, "The Scope and Results of Mothers' Classes," *NEA* (1903), 400-405; Helen L. Duncklee, "The Kindergartner and her Mothers' Meetings—VI," *Kindergarten Review*, X (March 1900), 397-401; Martha McMinn, "Problems of Mothers Lacking Wealth," *Kindergarten Magazine*, X (November 1897), 157-163; *Brooklyn Free Kindergarten Society Annual Report, 1930-1931*, 6-7; *Brooklyn Free Kindergarten Society Financial Report, 1925-1927*, 4-5; Jeanette L. Sturges, "Our Work for Foreigners in Chicago," *Home Mission Monthly*, XV (August 1901), 236-238; *New York Kindergarten Association Annual Report, 1918-1919*, 12.

26. For example, see Sturges, "Our Work for Foreigners in Chicago,"; *Brooklyn Free Kindergarten Society Annual Report, 1930-1931*, 6-7; *Silver Street Kindergarten Society Annual Report, 1896*, 15; *Louisville Free Kindergarten Association Annual Report, 1904-1905*, 27-28; *New York Kindergarten Association Annual Report, 1926-1927*, 9; Lucy Wheelock, "Kindergarten Clubs and Parent Teachers Associations," *Kindergarten Review*, XXVI (December 1915), 261-263.

27. "The Fourth Annual Convocation of Mothers," *Kindergarten Magazine*, X (November 1897), 164-178; Amalie Hofer, "National Congress of Mothers," *Kindergarten Magazine*, IX (February 1897), 439-448; Mary Dabney Davis, "A Century of the Kindergarten," *School Life*, XXII (November 1936), 67-68; "The First National Congress of Mothers," *Kindergarten Magazine*, IX (March 1897), 581-585.

28. Virginia T. Smith, "Minutes and Discussions," *NCCC* (1886), 382; Sarah B. Cooper, "Practical Results of Ten Years' Work," *NCCC* (1889), 191.

29. Nina C. Vandewalker, *The Kindergarten in American Education* (New York: The Macmillan Co., 1923), 63, 58-62; Amalie Hofer, "The Social Settlement and the Kindergarten," *Kindergarten Magazine*, VIII (September 1895), 54, 47-59; *Sixteenth Annual Report of the Golden Gate Kindergarten Association, 1895*, 29.

30. "Settlements and Settlement Kindergartens in New York City," *Kindergarten Magazine and Primary Digest* (May 1907), 610-615; Jane Addams, *Twenty Years at Hull House* (New York: The Macmillan Co., 1910), 102, 106; Allen F. Davis, *Spearheads for Reform* (New York: Oxford University Press, 1967), 43-44; Louise C. Wade, *Graham Taylor: Pioneer for Social Justice* (Chicago: University of Chicago Press, 1964), 121; Robert A. Woods and Albert J. Kennedy, *The Settlement Horizon* (New York: Russell Sage Foundation, 1922), 112, 132; Virginia E. Graeff, "The Elizabeth Peabody Kindergarten Settlement," *Kindergarten Review*, VIII (May 1898), 605-606; Elizabeth E. Manson, "The Ideas of a Kindergarten Settlement," *Kindergarten Review*, XIX (November 1908), 136-144; Caroline F. Brown, "Elizabeth Peabody House: The Kindergarten Settlement of Boston," *Kindergarten Review*, XII (October 1901), 63-67.

31. Woods and Kennedy, 131; Bertha Johnston, "The Chicago Kindergarten Institute," *Kindergarten Magazine*, XII (June 1900), 573-581; Woods and Kennedy, 115-116, 125, 412.

32. Lois Hufford, "Free Kindergarten Work in Indianapolis," *Kindergarten Magazine*, XI (January 1899), 305-313; *Annual Report of the Silver Street Kindergarten Society, 1895-1896*, 1-6.

33. Lillian D. Wald to Edgerton L. Winthrop, Jr., New York, February 13, 1905, Lillian D. Wald Papers, New York Public Library; Bertha Payne Newell, "Alice H. Putnam, 1841-1919," International Kindergarten Union Committee of Fifteen, *Pioneers of the Kindergarten in America* (New York: The Century Co., 1924).

34. Mrs. W. A. Allen, "The Stranger in our Midst," *Home Mission Monthly*, XXVII (March 1913), 113; "Practical Plans Bring Speedy Success," *Home Mission Monthly* (May 1904), 152.

35. *Annual Report of the Henshaw Free Kindergarten of Baltimore, 1902*, 3; Abell, *Urban Impact*, 143-144; *Tenth Annual Report of the Golden Gate Kindergarten Association, 1889*, 35; Mary Allen West, President of the Illinois W.C.T.U., "Annual Address," Alton, October 23, 1883, Sarah Cooper Papers, Cornell University; Vandewalker, *Kindergarten in American Education*, 103-107; *Eighth Annual Report of the Golden Gate Kindergarten Association, 1887*, 75; Anna E. Bryan, "Specific Temperance Lesson," *The Kindergarten*, I (November 1888), 221-222; Cora L. Stockham, "Total Abstinence," *The Kindergarten*, I (October 1888), 183-184.

36. Harrison, "Discussion," *NEA* (1892), 640.

CHAPTER IV

THE KINDERGARTEN AND TEACHER TRAINING

From the beginning, kindergartners in this country thought of themselves as professionals, their work requiring specialized training.[1] Pioneers like Susan Blow and Elizabeth Peabody considered at least one year of training essential, the better courses of study requiring two years for completion. According to them, neither sentimental concern for children nor practical teaching experience equipped one to conduct a kindergarten without a thorough knowledge of Froebelian principles. A few German emigrés, like Emma Marwedel and Maria Kraus-Boelte, who had studied with Froebel or his widow, taught many of the earliest courses, and as kindergartening became more popular, both charity associations and experienced individuals opened schools for prospective teachers. The kindergarten was also reflected in the growth of several normal schools and teachers' colleges.

In the 1880's, kindergartening provided a solution for many young women seeking a life outside the home. Although by that time many regarded teaching as "woman's natural profession," numerous girls still faced the choice of teaching and spinsterhood or marriage. While some exceptionally talented young women might seek careers in the fine arts, many traditional families still looked upon teaching as an undesirable way of life for their daughters.[2] Parents, however, often felt more at ease at the prospect of kindergartening, since the stress kindergartners laid on the responsibilities and beauties of motherhood contributed heavily to its general social as well as parental acceptability. It seemed to provide a woman with a vocation that purportedly would not subvert her maternal instincts. Maria Kraus, echoing Froebel, emphasized the need for nurses and mothers of all classes, for "all womanhood of every position in life," to understand and apply the kindergarten principles. In the same vein, William T. Harris regarded the St. Louis kindergarten experiment as beneficial, if only because Susan Blow had trained two hundred kindergartners likely to become knowledgeable as well as loving mothers.[3] At a National Educational Association convention in 1888, Kate Wiggin addressed her remarks to men who feared that any form of higher education for women made them "unfit" for their womanly duties. After chiding men for worrying too little about "weak-minded" women and too much about "strong-minded" ones, she reassured them that kindergarten training provided general as well as specific education for young women which made them not only

> better kindergartners, teachers and governesses, but better daughters, sisters, wives and mothers—yes, and sweeter, more cheerful old maids—simply because it made them better women.

She followed these remarks with a warning to men:

> No, my dear sirs, never tell us that our own work is wasted when we have, even in part, learned these things; but rather apply yourselves diligently to the creation of some sort of training school for young men or in fifty years there will be none good enough for our girls.[4]

As late as 1911, G. Stanley Hall felt that not only did the kindergarten provide an excellent opportunity for the young child to develop naturally, but, referring to the special rapport between women twenty-five to forty and young children, he said that kindergartening was an ideal occupation for women, keeping them young and happy while fulfilling the maternal instinct for those who did not marry. Furthermore, many people regarded going into slum areas and teaching in a charity kindergarten as a mission, doing God's service, and consequently, they even felt they had the Church's blessing. Thus, a young woman could begin to seek adventure without receiving censure from her family or society.[5]

As kindergartening became more acceptable and prevalent, the number of specialized training schools to accommodate the influx of young women increased; and, too, a few well-known normal schools introduced instruction in kindergartening, an event that had an im-

53

pact upon the teacher training in those particular schools. As early as 1870, Thomas Hunter, President of Manhattan's New York Normal College, made an abortive attempt at establishing a kindergarten in the College's model school. "Utterly disgusted with the barbarous system of restraint, ignorantly called 'discipline,' " Hunter resolved that with the opening of the College, he would find an alternate approach to activities in the classroom. After reading Froebel's ideas, he decided that the kindergarten was "the true foundation of all correct teaching," with its emphasis on the child's natural activities and its use of those activities for constructive purposes. Although the venture received complimentary publicity in *The New York Times*, this first kindergarten attempt deteriorated. There were several problems: the ages of the children between seven and eleven were wrong; Hunter failed to hire a suitable kindergartner or to procure a proper supply of materials; and the supervising principal of the kindergarten was not sympathetic to the notion of play in school. In 1874, however, when the Model School moved to a new building, Hunter succeeded in fulfilling all the elements of a Froebelian kindergarten, including a kindergartner trained by Maria Kraus, and he reported remarkable results. The kindergarten had ten times the number of children applying than could be accommodated, and it served as an experimental class for student teachers to expose them to Froebel's ideas about childhood. According to Hunter, the future teachers at the Normal College learned about child nature as they never could have from ordinary textbooks, and they were thus prepared to "enter upon their work with a loftier idea of their duties and responsibilities and with a broader humanity for the errors and miseries of their fellow-beings."[6]

Many of the training courses offered by prominent kindergartners attracted the attention of the better normal schools. For example, in 1883, Francis W. Parker, the new principal of Cook County Normal School near Chicago, revived the waning model kindergarten by asking Alice Putnam to teach her kindergarten training classes at the school. Colonel Parker had been familiar with Froebel's ideas for many years, both as principal of a normal school with a kindergarten in Dayton, Ohio, and as Superintendent of Schools in Quincy, Massachusetts, where he introduced Froebelian activities into the primary grades. Although Parker's pedagogy was influenced by other principles and approaches, Froebel's ideas contributed significantly to his overall philosophy. Parker regarded the kindergarten as the best foundation for the "new education," but when he requested funds from the Cook County Board of Education to pay Alice Putnam to teach kindergartening at the normal school, he ran into opposition from the Board.

Alice Putnam began her kindergarten activities in Chicago in 1874 when she started a study club in response to a letter received from Elizabeth Peabody urging parents to study Friedrich Froebel's ideas of early childhood. Over the next several years she enrolled in training courses and studied with Mrs. Anna J. Ogden in Columbus, Ohio, Susan Blow in St. Louis, Maria Kraus-Boelte in New York City, and Colonel Francis W. Parker for a summer course at Martha's Vineyard. By the time she attended Parker's course in 1880, she was already an experienced kindergartner and director of the recently organized Chicago Froebel Association Training School, which over the following thirty years trained over eight hundred kindergarten teachers. Putnam found Parker's ideas stimulating and significant, especially his ideas of applying Froebelian concepts in the elementary grades. She was subsequently instrumental in securing the principalship at Cook County Normal School for Parker in 1882. When the Board of Education rejected Parker's request to approve funds for teaching kindergartening, Putnam decided to teach without salary, while the Froebel Association paid the costs. In return, trainees from the normal school spent their practice teaching time assisting in the Association's charity kindergartens.[7]

Kindergarten training schools often formed the nucleus of a teachers' college, as in the case of Elizabeth Harrison's Chicago Kindergarten College. Elizabeth Harrison, who studied with Alice Putnam in Chicago, Susan Blow in St. Louis, Maria Kraus-Boelte in New York, and Baroness Marenholtz-Bulow in Europe, began teaching kindergartening in the private Loring School in Chicago. There among affluent families she took considerable pains to hold meetings to teach the mothers of her kindergarten children about Froebelian principles of education. One of the mothers in attendance, Mrs. John N. Crouse, realized the importance of educating all mothers this way, and she approached Elizabeth Harrison about setting up other mothers' classes in all parts of the city. With Crouse's help and financial backing, Harrison accepted the challenge and established several classes in which she attempted to explain and arouse women's deepest instincts of nurture and motherhood. She tried to dignify maternity, making women aware of their important responsibilities to their children. She also tried to help mothers understand the universality of their work and problems, since she found that mothers rich or poor shared many identical problems.[8]

The classes merged in 1886, with Mrs. Crouse's continued support, to create the Chicago Kindergarten College which offered both general mothers' classes and kindergarten training. Declaring child-rearing to be woman's "supreme vocation," the sponsors of the College intended their courses to teach women about the nature of the young child and how to best educate him. For example, in one of the classes conducted in the Mothers' Department, Elizabeth Harrison lectured on human nature in psychological and ethical terms using references to such writings as Emerson's poem, "The Days," Booker T. Washington's *Autobiography*, Froebel's books, and Susan Blow's *Commentaries*. For class discussion, Harrison wrote a series of booklets called "Questions on a Study of Child Nature" in which she delved into such topics as: "What is the intellectual value of training the senses? What does the habit of contrasting or comparing lead to? What is a perfect character? What is the proper diet for a child? How does nature educate your child?"[9] Harrison also provided intellectual stimulus for the mothers by inviting authors and educators to come speak at the College.

The "unique school for motherhood," as Susan Blow described it, was the first large scale effort to educate mothers in the ways of child nurture as Froebel had urged. The classes were well received and well attended, enrolling five thousand women in the decade 1886-1895. A former pupil recalled how Elizabeth Harrison had helped to set the fashion in the 1890's of "hitching one's wagon to a star." In those days, she said, "it was fashionable to have unbounded faith in the saving power of education as such, and of kindergarten training in particular. Those were the glorious pre-salary days," she continued sentimentally, "when one labored in and out of season for the love of the cause, when club members, mothers and daughters of the first families, wives of prominent ministers and officials, all enrolled for the study of child nurture under Miss Harrison's leadership."[10]

In her training classes for kindergartners Harrison expected hard work from her pupils and they, in turn, undertook ambitious projects, such as translating Froebel from the original German or composing music and stories. A memorial volume declared that Harrison allowed "no hidden ability or latent talent" of her students to lie fallow and demanded that they put their entire energies "into the service of childhood education." Her training school curriculum gradually expanded to a four year course of study requiring preparation in the social sciences, the humanities, sciences, and pedagogy, offering teacher preparation for the primary grades as well as the kindergarten. The school became known as the National College of Education in 1930.[11]

The contribution of the kindergarten to the growth of teaching institutions was reflected in yet another school, Teachers College, Columbia University. The origins of that college date back to 1880 with the formation of the Kitchen-Garden Association, a philanthropic organization which promoted Emily Huntington's system of domestic training. After visiting the kindergarten in the Henrietta Haines School, Emily Huntington had devised a system, known as the Kitchen-Garden, which explicitly imitated the kindergarten and substituted toy cups, brooms, and domestic utensils for the Froebelian gifts and occupations.[12] The system spread fairly rapidly, and in 1880, two years after Emily Huntington published *The Kitchen-Garden*, New York City alone had eleven such classes. Huntington conducted normal classes for those who wanted to teach Kitchen-Garden, and the Association laid heavy stress on the need for women to be properly trained before undertaking to teach. Inasmuch as Association members considered their system to be modeled on the kindergarten system, which required teachers to undergo a complete training course, they warned that "no one should attempt to teach Kitchen-Garden without having taken the whole course of Normal Class lessons."[13] In 1884, the Kitchen-Garden Association dissolved and reorganized as the Industrial Education Association, with broader aims of introducing industrial education into the public schools for boys and girls. In its Articles of Faith, the Association reasserted the Kitchen-Garden conviction that "the kindergarten system produced the best results with young children" and that their system merely extended Froebelian theory by adding industrial training to it and adapting its ideas to older children.[14]

The new Association's work expanded rapidly, and the need for appropriately trained public school teachers became more and more apparent. In 1887, it founded the New York College for the Training of Teachers with Nicholas Murray Butler as President. It opened with a five member faculty, one of whom taught kindergarten methods, and visiting lecturers. Two years later, the new institution received a charter under the name Teachers College.

Kindergartens contributed in still another way to the development of Teachers College with the establishment of an experimental school. Kindergarten training courses were traditionally operated in conjunction with a model kindergarten for purposes of observation and practice teaching. To this end, Mary Runyan, director of kindergarten work at Teachers College, made arrangements in 1899 to direct the charity kindergarten at St. Mary's Episcopal Church near campus. A few months later, the College, having been convinced of the advantages of the model kindergarten, arranged to open an elementary school located in the same parish house. In 1902, all the classes moved to a new building and formed the Speyer School. This school, particularly the kindergarten, served as a community center and remained open all day until ten o'clock at night almost every day of the year.[15]

A third kindergarten training school which formed the basis of a teachers' college was conducted by Lucy Wheelock in Boston. With the encouragement of Elizabeth Peabody and Dr. Henry Barnard, Wheelock opened her first training class in 1888 just after the Boston City Council voted to appropriate funds to incorporate kindergartens in the public school system and there arose a sudden need for well-trained, qualified teachers. Beginning with only six pupils, course enrollment grew rapidly at the Wheelock School. The curriculum broadened from a one year course in which Wheelock did most of the teaching, relying heavily on Froebel's *Mother-Play* and bringing in lecturers on psychology or art, to a two year course in 1895. The set of courses continually grew to include primary grades, nursery school, and more emphasis on psychology, arts, and sciences. Eventually, a newly reorganized four year course of study led to the accreditation of Wheelock College in 1944.

The growth of Lucy Wheelock's school clearly reflected her educational concepts. She brought in lecturers to acquaint the students with such current social and political issues as Americanization of immigrants and women's suffrage. She emphasized the significance of kindergartners working with mothers and the techniques of organizing meetings with them. Believing in the principle of continuity of education, she wanted to erase any gap between the kindergarten and primary grades, and she thus provided her future teachers with the goals and methods of teaching in all the early childhood years. Being among the first to appreciate pre-kindergarten education, Lucy Wheelock invited Abigail Eliot, the pioneer of nursery education in this country, to teach a course on the subject in 1925.

58

By 1929, all Wheelock School students took a three year course of study, receiving a nursery-kindergarten-primary diploma requiring courses, observation, and student teaching in all three areas.[16]

At least fifty normal schools in twenty-one states introduced kindergarten departments between 1890 and 1900, and there were indications that the new additions benefited future elementary school teachers as well as the kindergarten movement. Besides the testimony of such men as Thomas Hunter and Francis Parker, many students attested to the value of the kindergarten. In 1898, the director of the Milwaukee Normal School, Nina Vandewalker, sent questionnaires to 158 pupils not enrolled in the kindergarten course. Out of 130 replies, thirty had not had the time or opportunity to visit the kindergarten and therefore found it of no use. The others, however, judged their direct observation inspiring, thought-provoking, and helpful. They saw it as a good place to study not just the child's cognitive growth but his entire development. Vandewalker thus defended the presence of the kindergarten in a normal school on the grounds that it broadened a teacher's knowledge and experience, that it offered a better opportunity than the school for studying the child in action, and that it provided normal schools with an expression of naturalness and spontaneity, contrary to the "conservatism" of the school.[17]

Kindergarten training schools generally had admission procedures that were in many cases more selective than state normal schools. The Golden Gate Kindergarten Free Normal Training School, organized in July, 1891, continually raised its admission standards. Staffed with an impressive array of educators, including several professors from Stanford University, the training school received 120 applications in 1892 for its forty-eight openings. The school was able, therefore, to exercise a high degree of selectivity and to choose only the most talented and promising students. Specific entrance requirements to training classes varied. Some institutions like the California Training School, sponsored by the Silver Street Kindergarten Society, kept their requirements loose: a genuine love for children and interest in working and playing with them; musical ability; and a reasonably substantial educational background. Lucy Wheelock sought maturity and the equivalent of a high school diploma in her admission candidates. Others, however, had more rigorously defined prerequisites. For example, in 1894-1895, the training school of the Louisville Free Kindergarten Association sought college graduates who had to be over twenty years of age and to have studied physiology, physics, botany, zoology, and ancient, medieval, and modern history. Apparently the school could not maintain these standards, since ten years later it lowered the age minimum to eighteen years, but it still required at least a high school, preferably a college, diploma. Admission requirements to Elizabeth Harrison's Chicago Kindergarten College also included a high school diploma.[18]

In comparison, Oswego State Normal School in New York did not require high school diplomas of its applicants during the heyday of its pedagogical reputation in the 1880's. Entering Oswego students needed only to be sixteen years old, to be in good health, to have a certificate attesting to their good moral fiber, and to be able to pass an examination of basic subjects taught in elementary school. New York State normal schools did not require a high school diploma until 1895, and when the change came it caused a dramatic, if only temporary, drop in enrollment. At Cook County Normal School in 1883 the admission standard to the kindergarten training class was the same as the most advanced professional training class: at least three years of successful study in a first class high school. This requirement changed the following year to a high school or college diploma.[19]

Kindergarten training schools usually divided their program into one year of course work and observation and a second year of practice teaching. The courses included principles and methods of instruction, music, mathematics, art, ethics, literature, and a variety of other offerings, drawing on the strengths of the individual teacher. According to some training school notebooks, future kindergartners, in studying Froebel's gifts and the principles and rules governing their use, dealt with such questions as the importance of the child's studying forms in order to think of things in terms of their possibilities and limitations, while satisfying "the marked instincts of the child . . . to investigate and . . . to transform."[20] Trainees learned basic geometry in order to understand the meaning of terms like angles, trapezoids, and rhomboids and to be able to use them in creating designs. They spent countless hours filling notebooks with different series of patterns made with the gifts. One sequence, for example, using the third gift, a cube divided into eight smaller cubes, involved the story of "The Three Bears." The cubes could be used to build the house, the open door, the table, and the three chairs, cereal bowls and beds.[21]

Also during their instruction, students undertook a formal investigation of color which was supposed not only to gratify the aesthetic sense of the future kindergartner, but to familiarize her with the laws of color and harmony. This was so that she might in turn "direct the child's natural instinct for harmony and develop in him a love for pure and beautiful color and an appreciation or feeling for the beautiful harmony of nature's combinations."[22] The trainee used her knowledge of geometric design and laws of color with her own aesthetic sense to fashion page after page of designs of paper weaving, cutting and folding, and sewing with wool on cardboard. The painstaking care evidently required in these compositions might have discouraged any but the most enthusiastic student.[23] Elizabeth Harrison's diary, kept while attending Maria Kraus's training school in New York City, alluded to the hard and unimaginative work required of her, such as copying and completing the Kraus "Schools of Work," which consisted partially of "130 mat-weaving 'patterns,' 700 paper folding forms—300 paper cutting forms, 14 books of linear drawings. . . ." The purpose of these assignments, she remarked ironically, was to learn "the power that the genuine play spirit could gain in leading the children aright into the joy of creative activity, guided into worth-while experiences."[24] It would seem that only the inspiration of the training teacher, Froebel's principles, and personal motivation kept the faith and conviction of these young kindergartners in the face of such demands.

Training class instructors expected their students to have some kind of ability in music and story-telling, a facet of education little appreciated by normal schools. During the first few years of kindergartening in this country, there was a paucity of children's songs. Those that existed came from a translation of Froebel's *Mutter und Köse Lieder*, but they were awkward and had lost much of their meaning in translation. Consequently, kindergartners filled the void by inventing new songs, stories, and games, always containing a moral or a purpose. Kindergartner Emily Poulsson published a book in 1889 filled with songs and stories requiring children to imitate their teacher's hand motions while singing. For example, in "The Counting Lesson," the song goes:

> Here is the beehive. Where are the bees?
> Hidden away where nobody sees.
> Soon they come creeping out of the hive—
> One!—two!—three!—four!—five!
> etc.[25]

The children indicate the beehive with a closed fist and the bees by number with their fingers. Patty Smith Hill wrote a song called "Happy Birthday to You," a song to be commonly known by generations of children. Years later while attending a Broadway show, she heard her copyrighted song used without her permission. She successfully sued the producer, using the money for nursery and kindergarten projects. In referring to the song books written by kindergartners between 1878 and 1910, Patty Hill claimed that:

> With all of our musical faults musicians realize that we were among the first educators to appreciate the poetic value in song, and that, as a body, we have provided more good songs for little children than all other educators and musicians put together.[26]

Kindergartner Kate Wiggin wrote many popular children's books and stories, including *Rebecca of Sunnybrook Farm*, *Timothy's Quest*, and *The Birds' Christmas Carol*, creating characters based on many of the children in her kindergartens. Her internationally popular books were translated into eight foreign languages: German, Polish, Danish, Swedish, Dutch, French, Bohemian, and Japanese.[27]

Despite the highly stylized format of much of the training curriculum, students had more direct and less academic opportunity to learn about kindergartening from observing their master teacher conduct a kindergarten and from a follow-up period of questions and discussion. Although at that time most normal schools did not include learning from observation, it played an important role in kindergarten training. We know from Elizabeth Harrison's school diary that as she watched Maria Kraus-Boelte teach kindergarten she marvelled at how the children maintained their interest in an activity for as long as an hour at a stretch without wearying. In another entry that term, she noted the "willing obedience and entire satisfaction of the children," and she determined to learn her teacher's secret. Kraus-Boelte said simply to be genuine and natural with the children at all times. For example, she urged Elizabeth and the rest of her trainees not to use fake flowers in dirt and call that a real garden and not to bring in stuffed animals to be petted as if they were alive. If no facilities for a garden existed, then she suggested bringing in a few leaves or a cut flower to teach children about nature. Similarly, she strongly objected to the idea of dressing children up in elaborate costumes for plays and games, maintaining that the spirit for such activities should not be superficial but should come from the mind and heart of the child.[28]

Pupils studying with the Krauses' New York Normal Kindergarten had the opportunity to observe other kindergartners. Elizabeth Harrison reported having visited the kindergarten run by the Ethical Culture Society. There the students found a beautiful building complete with modern conveniences and witnessed the day's activities, after which they had a long talk with the director, Dr. Hamburger. Later, Maria Kraus-Boelte and the pupils exchanged their observations in class.[29]

The existing training schools could not prepare enough kindergartners for the growing number of kindergartens. Indeed by 1898, a committee of the International Kindergarten Union saw this as a major problem. The committee members saw that many inexperienced kindergartners had to train their own assistants, which led them to warn that many criticisms leveled at kindergartens were "frequently the direct outcome of the immaturity of the teacher." Well-trained kindergartners were needed everywhere, and graduates of the best schools were in demand. Louise Taft, an organizer of the Cincinnati Free Kindergarten Association and mother of President William Howard Taft, felt fortunate to receive a letter from Susan Blow stating that although she had to decline their offer to come to Cincinnati, she would send one of her training school graduates to run their class. The Golden Gate Kindergarten Training School, like others, sent its graduates all over the country as well as abroad.[30]

The good training classes were always filled, because thorough preparation continued to be the hallmark of the excellent kindergartner. Not only neophytes, but experienced kindergartners as well, travelled great distances seeking different authorities in an effort to enrich and stimulate their understanding of Froebel, children, psychology, and philosophy. During the course of her career, Kate Wiggin studied with Emma Marwedel in Los Angeles; William Hailmann in Indianapolis; Elizabeth Peabody and Mary J. Garland in Boston; Alice Putnam in Chicago; and Susan Blow in St. Louis. Elizabeth Harrison, as already noted, studied with many of the same teachers, and in addition travelled abroad to learn from Baroness Marenholtz-Bulow. The director of the Golden Gate Kindergarten Association Training School travelled east in 1892 to visit kindergartens and to attend "a course of *Special* Instruction in Chicago."[31]

Teacher preparation for kindergartners was always considered important in order to maintain high standards in kindergarten work. Its excellence influenced normal schools, which began to incorporate kindergarten courses into their curriculum. Such courses introduced educational innovation to future elementary school teachers. The rigorous entrance requirements for admission to a good kindergarten training school also influenced the entrance standards of the normal schools. Most important, in the last decades of the nineteenth century, the kindergarten movement alerted normal schools and later teachers' colleges to the significance of understanding the growth of child development.

1. This is in contrast to the experience in the field of social work, where formal training marked the critical difference between the careers of paid and volunteer workers. See Roy Lubove, *The Professional Altruist* (Cambridge: Harvard University Press, 1965), 41.

2. See Andrew Sinclair, *The Better Half* (New York: Harper and Row, 1965), 9-12, 100; Thomas Woody, *History of Women's Education in the United States*, II (New York: Science Press, 1929), 461-463; Robert A. Smuts, *Women and Work in America* (New York: Columbia University Press, 1959), 38-39.

3. Maria Kraus-Boelte, "The Kindergarten and the Mission of Women," *National Educational Association Journal of Addresses and Proceedings* (1887), 209 (Hereinafter cited as *NEA*); William T. Harris, "Superintendent's Report," *Annual Report of the St. Louis Public Schools, 1879-1880*, 222.

4. Kate Douglas Wiggin, "Discussion," *NEA* (1888), 357-358.

5. G. Stanley Hall, *Educational Problems*, Vol. I (New York: D. Appleton and Co., 1911), 6-7; Marguerite N. Bell, *With Banners: A Biography of Stella L. Wood* (St. Paul, Minn.: Macalester College Press, 1954), 21-24.

6. Thomas Hunter, "The Kindergarten in Normal Training," *American Journal of Education*, XXXI (1881), 197-200; "Normal Education in New York and Brooklyn," *New York Times*, March 7, 1871, 4:3.

7. Jack K. Campbell, *Colonel Francis W. Parker: Children's Crusader* (New York: Teachers College Press, 1967), 106-107, 118, 129-146; Francis W. Parker, "Cook County Normal School, 1883-1884," *Report of the Superintendent of Public Instruction of the State of Illinois, 1882-1884*, 35-38; "Alice Putnam," *Notable American Women, 1607-1950*, III (Cambridge: Harvard University Press, Belknap Press, 1971), 105-106. For more information on kindergarten training in Chicago see Thomas Woody, *History of Women's Education*, II, 459; Madame Marie Blanc, *The Condition of Woman in the United States: A Traveller's Notes* (Boston: Roberts Bros., 1895), 46; George S. Counts, *School and Society in Chicago* (New York: Harcourt, Brace, and Co., 1928), 206-209; Constance Mackenzie, "Free Kindergartens," *National Conference on Charities and Correction Proceedings* (1886), 49.

8. Elizabeth Harrison, "The Scope and Results of Mothers' Classes," *NEA* (1903), 403-404; Edna Dean Baker, "A Tribute to Elizabeth Harrison," *Social Progress*.

VII (December 1923), 374; Elizabeth Harrison," *Notable American Women*, II, 147-149.

9. Elizabeth Harrison, "Shop Windows," Chicago Kindergarten College, December 12, 1900, 23-24, Archives of the Association for Childhood Education International, Washington, D.C. (Hereinafter cited as ACEI); Elizabeth Harrison, *Questions on a Study of Child Nature: No. 2—Mothers' Classes* (Chicago: Chicago Kindergarten College, 1897), 8-9.

10. Susan E. Blow, "Kindergarten Education," in Nicholas Murray Butler, *Education in the United States* (New York: American Book Co., 1910), 43; *In Memoriam: Elizabeth Harrison*, statement of the National Kindergarten and Elementary College, ACEI.

11. *In Memoriam*, ACEI; Baker, "A Tribute," 375; "Elizabeth Harrison," *Notable American Women*, II, 147-149. Before 1930, the name of the institution had been changed a few times: 1912, the National Kindergarten College; 1917, the National Kindergarten and Elementary College.

12. Emily Huntington, *How to Teach Kitchen-Garden* (New York: Doubleday, Page and Co., 1901), 14-15. For specific examples of lessons, see Huntington, *The Kitchen-Garden* (New York: Schermerhorn, 1878).

13. *Annual Report of the Kitchen-Garden Association, 1880*, 5-7, and *1882*, 6-7; Lawrence Cremin, et al., *A History of Teachers College*, Columbia University (New York: Columbia University Press, 1954), 12-14.

14. Walter L. Hervey, "Historical Sketch of Teachers College," *Teachers College Record* (1900), 14, 19; Cremin, *Teachers College*, 10-42; James Earl Russell, *Founding Teachers College* (New York: Columbia University Press, 1937), 3-20.

15. Russell, *Founding Teachers College*, 59; Cremin, *Teachers College*, 104-105.

16. *The Wheel*, Yearbook of Wheelock School, Fiftieth Anniversary Edition, 1939; Winifred E. Bain, *Leadership in Childhood Education* (Boston: Wheelock College Bureau of Publication, 1964), 12-41; Lucy Wheelock, "The Wheelock School," *Childhood Education*, III (October 1926), 88-90; "Lucy Wheelock," in *Dictionary of American Biography*, Supplement Four (New York: Charles Scribners Sons, 1974), 874-875.

17. Nina C. Vandewalker, *Kindergarten in American Education* (New York: The Macmillan Co., 1923), 199-200; Nina C. Vandewalker, "The Influence of the Kindergarten Spirit Upon a Normal School," *Kindergarten Magazine*, X (March 1898), 427-433.

18. *Sixteenth Annual Report of the Golden Gate Kindergarten Association, 1892*, 2; Sarah Cooper to Hattie Skilton, San Francisco, June 19, 1892, and Earl Barnes to Sarah Cooper, May 9, 1892, Sarah Cooper Papers, New York State Regional Archives, Cornell University (Hereinafter cited as SC/CU); *Silver Street Kindergarten Society Annual Report, 1895-1896*, 6; *Louisville Free Kindergarten Association Annual Reports: 1894-1895* and *1904-1905*; Thomas Cushing, *Historical Sketch of Chauncey-Hall School, 1828-1894* (Boston: Clapp, 1895), 67-70; Editors, "Miss Harrison and the Chicago Kindergarten College," *Kindergarten Magazine*, V (June 1893), 744.

19. Dorothy Rogers, *Oswego* (New York: Appleton-Century-Crofts, 1961), 59-60; Francis W. Parker, "Cook County Normal School," *Report of the Superintendent of Public Instruction of the State of Illinois, 1884-1886*, 30-33.

20. F. Maud Berry, "Notebook, 1900-1902," ACEI.

21. Kate Kempland, "Training School Notebook," and Susie Andrew's notebook: "Froebel Kindergarten, 1908, Fannie A. Smith Kindergarten Training School," ACEI.

22. F. Maud Berry, "Color Harmony Notebook," n.d. [1901?], ACEI.

23. Gertrude Coy, "Weaving," "Paper Cutting," and "Sewing" books, Duluth, Minnesota, n.d., ACEI.

24. Elizabeth Harrison, "School Diary, 1883", 1. See, for example, Susan S. Harriman, "Early Days at Wheelock," *The Wheel*, 1939, 92-93, and "Alumnae Letters," 94-96.

25. Emily Poulsson, *Finger Plays* (Boston: Lothrop, Lee and Shepard Co., 1889), 54-56. (Reissued by Dover Press.)

26. Patty Smith Hill, "The History of the Kindergarten Song in America," *Kindergarten-Primary Magazine*, XXIII (January 1911), 142; Margaret Rasmussen, "Over the Editor's Desk," *Childhood Education*, XXXVII (March 1961), 352-353.

27. Kate Douglas Wiggin, *My Garden of Memory* (Boston: Houghton Mifflin Co., 1923), 333, 445-447.

28. Elizabeth Harrison, "School Diary," January 29, February 7, and March 16, 1883, ACEI.

29. *Ibid.*, June 11, 1883.

30. Alice Putnam, "The International Kindergarten Union Waxes Strong," *Kindergarten Magazine*, X (April 1898), 532-533; Susan Blow to Louise Taft, Farmington, December 7 and December 16, 1879, Taft Family Papers, Series I, Library of Congress, Washington, D.C.; Sarah Cooper to Hattie Skilton, San Francisco, January 13 and August 3, 1894, SC/CU.

31. Sarah Cooper to Hattie Skilton, San Francisco, June 19, 1892, SC/CU.

CHAPTER V

THE KINDERGARTEN AND
EDUCATIONAL REFORM

By the end of the 1890's, the idea of the kindergarten was widely accepted by the American public. It was a popular form of philanthropic, missionary, and settlement activity. School boards in many cities, like St. Louis, Indianapolis, Boston, Chicago, and Philadelphia, had included kindergartens in their public school systems, while other cities were getting ready to take the plunge. Moreover, the most respected normal schools had kindergarten departments, and the department at Teachers College, Columbia University, made it possible for teachers of preschoolers to graduate with college diplomas. Numerous statements reiterated the position that the kindergarten was no longer on trial. For example, in 1893 the *Century Magazine* editors felt that critics and detractors needed to defend their objections, not vice versa, since the kindergarten had received the "almost unanimous approval of experts" and the "enthusiastic endorsement" from that part of the general public which availed itself of the opportunity to understand its purpose and methods.[1]

As the editorial suggested, the kindergarten, in addition to its general acceptance, also captured the interest of such leading experimental and progressive educators as Francis Parker, G. Stanley Hall, and John Dewey. American institutionalization of Froebelian ideas, the publicity surrounding these endeavors, and the growing numbers of people involved in them prepared much of the groundwork for what people around the turn of the century called the "new" education. Indeed, leaders of this "new" movement freely acknowledged their intellectual debt to Froebel. Without attempting to enumerate or analyze all the various themes and influences contributing to the development of what is loosely defined as "progressive" education, it can clearly be said that many of the basic tenets of that pedagogy, such as the child-centered approach, the significance of play, the use of toys as educational materials, and the idea of the classroom as an embryonic social community, lay deeply imbedded in kindergarten theory and practice. Furthermore, although divisions appeared among kindergartners as to how strictly teachers had to adhere to Froebel's original system, even the most traditional teachers in the movement had innovative ideas to impart to American pedagogy in the late nineteenth and early twentieth centuries.

John Dewey lauded Friedrich Froebel as having been the first to consciously set forth three crucial principles. First, he admired the fact that the German innovator rooted all his pedagogy in the activity of the child and that he understood the significance and educational value of play. Dewey said that in this way Froebel showed that "the spontaneous activities of children, plays, games . . . previously ignored as trivial, futile, or even condemned as positively evil . . ." were "the foundation-stones of educational method." Second, the young educational reformer applauded the principle that children should learn cooperative social behavior and how to live with one another in school. And third, he recognized the validity of the notion that children, as well as adults, secure "valuable knowledge" through productive and creative activities. Dewey, himself, adopted the term "occupations" from the kindergarten to describe some of the activities he devised for the child.[2]

G. Stanley Hall, considered the father of the child-study movement, credited Froebel with developing a system based on play as a salient activity for children, but Hall also praised the German pioneer for being the first to point out the racial recapitulation theory, which, according to Hall, was a basic theory of genetic psychology. "Each successive generation and each successive individual," Froebel had written in 1829, goes "through the entire pattern of earlier human development." Similarly, Hall agreed with Froebel that there are stages in a child's development which adults should respect and which educational organization should take into account. In this vein, Froebel had written that he saw life as "a con-

68

stant and progressive process of becoming, a continuous advance towards an infinite goal from one stage to another" and he thought it was "inexpressibly harmful to regard the development and education of man as a static isolated process . . ." Hall additionally praised Froebel's recognition of the need for children to play outdoors as much as possible. Thus, although Hall also made criticisms of several kindergarten practices and procedures, he still, with uncharacteristic humility, wrote that he considered himself a "true disciple" of Froebel and called him "the morning star of the child study movement."[3]

Hall began his research in child study by comparing kindergarten children to those who had not attended, and he as well as others in the field continued to regard the kindergarten as the best place to carry on their research because of the pupils' freedom of expression. In 1880, Hall conducted a survey in Boston of children just beginning first grade entitled "The Contents of Children's Minds Upon Entering School." Pauline Shaw supplied him with four of her best kindergartners to act as his questioners, and the results indicated that children who had attended kindergarten showed more familiarity with concepts and objects than other children. Sometimes Hall's penchant for exact measurement got out of hand, as in 1893 when he suggested the following procedure with utter seriousness: take two or three children out at a time and measure every part of them, using calipers for the diameter of the head and body, tape measures for height and circumference, scales for weight, and special instruments for teeth, eyes, nose, ears, throat, and movement.[4] Other students of childhood education thought the kindergarten an ideal opportunity for studying a child's aesthetic and social nature because of the games and artistic endeavors of the youngsters. As children played they could also observe the nature of the interaction of individual temperament, sex, age, nationality, and environment, as well as the course of physical development, especially in terms of motor and constructive abilities.[5] Dewey particularly asked all kindergartners and their assistants to examine carefully the spontaneous activities of children, pointing out that few other persons had the opportunity to make such observations.[6]

The kindergarten movement always had innovative people within its ranks who did not follow Froebel's precise system but worked out variations. For example, in Chicago in the 1880's Alice Putnam, who was thoroughly versed in Froebelian theory, never allowed herself to be bound to exact methodology. She used a quotation from Froebel as her motto: "Do this and see to what knowledge it leads thee," and she told her training classes that she did not need elaborate equipment, but could conduct a kindergarten in a meadow with just the children, nature, and herself. Another critic of slavish adherence to a precise method, William Hailmann, reminded kindergarten teachers that: "the child, not the first or second gift is to be developed." He complained of "too much schoolishness in our kindergarten: time tables, sequences, laws of opposites, logical development and the like." Other kindergartners, as we have already seen, like Kate Smith Wiggin and Emily Poulsson, wrote new books of stories, games, and songs for children to avoid sole reliance on Froebel's *Mutter Und Köse Lieder*. Lucy Wheelock, while choosing to preserve what she considered to be the best aspects of the Froebelian kindergarten, urged her pupils to update their programs with the most important and significant current educational discoveries or theories.[7]

By the turn of the twentieth century, a growing number of educators had chosen to operate under the premise that Froebel had devised the kindergarten in order to illustrate his general educational ideas and that for teachers to accept all aspects of his program as final was antithetical to Froebel's spirit and real intentions. Many argued that since Froebel had utilized all the philosophical and psychological understanding available in his day, Froebel no doubt would have welcomed the opportunity to criticize and reevaluate his program on the basis of new knowledge in these fields.

For one thing, nineteenth-century faculty psychology, on which Froebel had depended, had by the end of that century fallen from favor. This earlier philosophy held that the mind possessed a few general abilities or faculties, such as memory, attention, or reason, which functioned in the same way for all kinds of people, while the newer theory suggested that the mind had many separate functions which were in some ways related, but whose relatedness was exaggerated in faculty psychology. According to Edward L. Thorndike, the "new psychology" regarded the mind as "a well-nigh infinite multitude of special capacities or habits, or functions, each of which is related closely to only a few others and is related to the majority hardly at all." Thus, although Dewey strongly recommended that all teachers study Froebel's substantial contributions to early childhood education, he still felt that current understanding of child psychol-

70

ogy, gained in part in the kindergarten, demanded "emancipation from the necessity of following any . . . prescribed . . . sequences of gifts, plays or occupations."[8]

Ideas and methods stemming from the child-study movement increasingly reached kindergartners through summer courses at Chautauqua or at such universities as Chicago, Colorado, and Clark. Many of the ideas set forth in the classes were familiar, of course: children should be studied for what they were and not considered small or immature adults, all aspects in their natures—physical and psychological as well as intellectual—were important. But some of the ideas reflected in scientific child study stressed continuous observation, experiment, and reevaluation, and some kindergartners refused to accept this challenge. In the summer of 1895, thirty-five kindergartners attended a course held by Professors G. Stanley Hall and William S. Burnham at Clark University. In the first lecture, Hall expressed basic approval of Froebel's system, but also called Susan Blow "the Pope" of the kindergarten movement and sharply criticized her insistence upon certain activities, such as the use of very small materials. Recent studies, he pointed out, had indicated that when young children were forced to use their small muscles which had not yet been fully developed physically and to use their eyes in such intense close work, it caused tension and nervousness. Insulted, thirty-three out of thirty-five teachers indignantly stalked out, leaving in the class only Patty Smith Hill of Louisville, Kentucky, and Anna Bryan, her former training teacher. These two women, who contributed extensively to reconstructing the kindergarten program, felt that the conferences they held with Hall and Burnham that summer had really introduced them "to the new child study movement, to the necessity for changing materials, curricula, and methods in the light of newer knowledge about both physical and mental health."[9]

Increasingly, however, kindergartners became more receptive to, and even took an active role in advocating change in the kindergarten curriculum. Not only did more of them enroll in summer school courses in child study, but many teachers began to be more selective in their use of the gifts and occupations. They retained the building gifts but enlarged them, and introduced additional materials for the occupations, such as paper and paste, boxes, cloth, string, wood, nails, and anything else three-dimensional, plastic, and adaptable to the unskilled hand of the young child. Some allowed more free play

71

during recesses and special periods, and others tried using a core curriculum for a given period of time.[10] Many kindergartners objected to sole reliance for subject matter upon material from Froebel's *Mutter und Köse Lieder, Mother-Play*, which had been the Bible of early kindergartners and which contained stories and activities based on the needs and environment in early nineteenth-century rural Germany. Instead of teaching a child about courage by having him play games about knights and castles, many kindergartners chose to use more relevant models, like firemen and policemen. It seemed perfectly ridiculous to some to insist upon using Froebel's games and songs about winter and snow with California children who had never seen or felt snow.[11] By changing kindergarten activities to ground them in the child's realm of reality, many teachers thus hoped to avoid the formalism, abstraction, and symbolism which they said resulted from transporting Froebel's songs and games to American urban kindergartens.

In addition, many kindergartners warned that sometimes the humane educational purposes got lost in technicalities, and they expressed alarm when teachers seemed more concerned with particular materials, gifts, songs, or symbolism than with the children.[12] Those with a freer attitude toward Froebel's precise system enjoyed and frequently referred to Grace Owen's 1906 article which stated that research into the programs in Froebel's original kindergartens revealed no evidence of exactness, no daily or weekly syllabus. Although there was some directed work, she concluded that Froebel's program appeared to have been "simple and informal" and his subject matter, such as animals, shepherds, and beehives, was drawn from the German child's immediate experience. Kindergartners, she argued, ought to return to Froebel's more informal and natural approach to the curriculum.[13]

Articles in such journals as the *Kindergarten Magazine* also reflected the growing experimentation. One writer, for example, stressed the important kindergarten precept that in all phases of education it is best to "incorporate *doing* as far as possible at every step" and that the doing should involve physical, mental, and emotional activities. Another article urged teachers to make practical use of the results of scientific child study: newly devised eye and ear tests could determine physical defects, and physiological studies showed that the optimal period of mental effort for a child was forty-five minutes followed by ten minutes of physical activity.

Editorials called for openness toward new ideas. For example, Andrea and Amalie Hofer, editors of the *Kindergarten Magazine* in 1893, advised their readers that:

> This is the day of growth and of growing, and premature or final conclusions do not find place therein. Every teacher, every kindergartner, every parent has a right to test the newer method born of yesterday's experience and of every today's necessity.[14]

There were those who could not accept any tampering with the traditional system and, led by Susan Blow, they refuted criticisms of their materials, symbolism, and conception of the child. Miss Blow saw the threat of a growing divisiveness among kindergartners, and in a letter to Kate Wiggin just after the turn of the century she explained:

> Forty years have changed the kindergarten from a consecrated vocation to a profession. It was the spirit of the pioneer work which was sacred and exalted. They were the glorious days when we never knew whether the kindergarten would last overnight, and never doubted that it would last forever. How to renew and perpetuate that spirit is the one problem of the Kindergarten Movement.[15]

Ironically, she attempted to solve that problem by trying to commit other kindergartners to accept her own authoritative interpretation of Froebel and the kindergarten curriculum.[16]

The tide, however, was against such a strictly orthodox interpretation, and even in public school kindergartens where there were more constraints, teachers began to use experimental approaches. Susan Blow, fearing the trend, wrote to Fanniebelle Curtis, her confidante, and the supervisor of kindergartens in Brooklyn:

> *Now* something must be done to get practical work conformed to Froebelian ideals. The type of kindergarten which exists more or less perfectly in Brooklyn, Philadelphia, Boston, Pittsburgh, St. Louis, Baltimore, Washington, etc., etc., must conquer the *type* of kindergarten represented by the N.Y. Public Kindergartens.[17]

Under the supervision of Dr. Jenny Merrill, New York City kindergartners experimented with new activities and revised their programs in response to the children's needs. Dr. Merrill recommended that teachers keep a separate book for each child containing a photograph, family history, and notes on his behavior during the first few days, and then record weekly as much information as possible. She also suggested keeping a book with lesson plans on the left side and comments about pupil reaction on the right side, for use in evaluating the program. She reminded her kindergartners that observation of behavior and analysis of drawings could be an effective means of understanding individuals. In other cities, like Newton, Massachusetts, Richmond, Indiana, and Des Moines, Iowa, kindergartners selectively discarded the old gifts and experimented with larger or new ones. In Boston, Laura Fisher, a student of Susan Blow who remained generally sympathetic to her mentor, reported that kindergartens tried using such new materials as sand and sand-tables, extra or "collateral" materials to illustrate topics, and enlarged blocks. From Milwaukee, Stella Heinemann wrote in 1906; "Our kindergartens are in every way progressive." Years previously, they had carefully hired the most excellent teachers available and had revised their kindergarten program, jettisoning the old sequence work.[18]

The internal conflict among personalities and ideologies within the kindergarten movement raged particularly on two fronts: at some of the meetings of the International Kindergarten Union and on the faculty of Teachers College, Columbia University. The I.K.U., founded in 1892, broadened the work of the National Educational Association kindergarten department by involving different groups and people. It was, in short, an attempt to achieve "combined action" in the place of "isolated effort." Because of the controversy among kindergarten leaders about modification of Froebel's original ideas, the International Kindergarten Union voted in 1903 to have a committee of fifteen, later expanded to nineteen, issue a comprehensive statement of Froebelian principles. As the committee held its meetings, discussion revealed that the members could not agree on a single report, and they finally chose to write three separate reports, chaired by Susan Blow, Patty Hill, and Elizabeth Harrison respectively. For Blow, the nine years during which the committee had annual meetings to discuss issues relating to the kindergarten were a real crusade. In May, 1909, she urged her friend, Fanniebelle Curtis, to recuperate from her illness quickly so that she could help write the report: "We shall all be needed to carry it to a triumphant issue. Be good to yourself as a way of being good to the cause." In 1910, she wrote that she hoped to train a new group of leaders in her New York class anticipating that "then we shall go from victory to victory."[19] Predictably, the main differences in the actual reports published in 1913 centered around issues already touched upon in this chapter. Kindergartners were then free to think through Blow's insistence upon a Uniform Program for all kindergartens, Hill's view of the kindergarten program "as a flexible plan of action," or Harrison's moderate view which maintained some of the old while inviting some innovation.

One of the three signers of Harrison's moderate report was Lucy Wheelock, President of the International Kindergarten Union from 1895-1899 and then chairman of the Committee of Nineteen and editor of their reports. Wheelock, like Harrison, believed in evolutionary changes in Froebel's system, but she objected to discarding too much too soon. The early kindergartners, she remarked, may have become too devoted to Froebel and his writings, but it had been necessary for them to stick closely to the Froebelian instruction in order to learn it thoroughly. She reminded critics of the unbounded enthusiasm that existed in the early days when the pioneer kindergartners saw Froebel's kindergarten "as a means of regeneration of mankind." Finding herself in the role of mediator during much of the controversy, she urged kindergartners to return to Froebel's most basic kindergarten creed: "A child is a plant in a garden, needing understanding care and guidance."[20]

At Teachers College, the kindergarten department proved to be a strong center of innovation. The climate of opinion there is apparent in the point of view expressed by James Earl Russell, Dean of Teachers College from 1897 to 1927, as well as in the faculty he recruited and in the courses offered in that department. Russell declared in 1904 that kindergarten training on a university level must embrace a range of subjects, including philosophy of education, child study, and child development, and that all phases of the kindergarten must be scrutinized, analyzed, and criticized if the kindergarten were to become more than a philanthropic institution.[21]

In 1905, Dean Russell invited Patty Smith Hill to come to Teachers College to lecture on the newer methods in kindergartening; in so doing he secured for his faculty the most important kindergartner who would lock horns with Susan Blow. Patty Hill had grown up in Louisville, Kentucky, in a family of six children. Her father, a Princeton graduate and a Presbyterian minister, had also served as the president of a woman's college, as the headmaster of a girls' school, and as an editor. Dismayed that so many young women seemed to marry for financial security alone, he encouraged his daughters as

75

well as his sons to pursue careers. In 1887, Patty enrolled in a new class run by Anna Bryan in Louisville to teach young ladies about Froebelian kindergartens. After graduation, Anna Bryan gave her pupil the responsibility for running the training class's demonstration kindergarten and urged her to regard it as an educational laboratory. When Bryan delivered a provocative lecture at the National Educational Association convention in 1890, Patty Hill accompanied her and helped to illustrate some of their new ideas. Word began to circulate about their classes, where they did not dictate sequences and designs to children but let them create their own, and over three thousand visitors came to Louisville to observe their kindergartens. In 1893, however, Anna Bryan returned to her home city of Chicago to work with the Free Kindergarten Association, and Patty Hill taught the training classes in Louisville until 1905 when she left to go to Teachers College. During the years in Louisville, however, she travelled extensively during the summers to study under the new experimental educators. She worked with Colonel Francis Parker at the Cook County Normal School, with John Dewey at the University of Chicago, and with G. Stanley Hall and William Burnham at Clark University.[22]

When Patty Hill came to Teachers College, Susan Blow was lecturing there. In kindergartening generally, Blow's orthodox interpretation of Froebel had begun to lose ground to the new child psychology, to Dewey's instrumentalism, and to widespread attacks on any kind of formalism. Dean Russell knew he needed an experienced and creative person to apply the newer thought expertly to the kindergarten, and Patty Hill seemed the perfect choice. Guided by Anna Bryan's favorite text, "The letter killeth but the spirit giveth light," Hill embarked upon a long and productive career at Teachers College continuing with her experiments in preschool education for several decades. Her lectures in 1905 were so popular that the following year Dr. Russell appointed her director of the newly formed training classes for supervisors. For several decades she continued her experiments in preschool education, branching out from the kindergarten to nursery school and community center projects. She was widely respected at Teachers College. She became a full professor, received an honorary degree of Doctor of Letters, and after retirement was one of the first women to be honored with the title Professor Emeritus from Columbia University.[23]

Patty Hill credited Froebel with emphasizing the need to provide a natural, healthy, and aesthetic surrounding for children because of the impressionability of youngsters and the ease with which they absorbed ideas and behavior from their environment. In following Froebel's ideas, she said, kindergartners had made significant contributions to American education by stressing the need for beautiful rooms and school grounds, excursions, music, games, and well-educated and well-prepared teachers. She observed that in the early days of the pioneer stages the kindergarten was such a happy place compared to the public school room that primary teachers did not even consider it an educational institution. While the kindergarten movement in the United States had once been fifty years ahead of its time, by the time it won both public and educational acceptance *rigor mortis* had set in and kindergarten procedure had become rigid and formalized. Characterizing this latter period as the time when "the kindergarten fell in love with itself," she believed the assertion that Froebel used his materials in a natural innovative manner in his daily contact and relationships with children, but that they had become stylized and formal as he had spent time teaching adults about his ideas. She considered it necessary to return to a more fluid procedure in the classroom in order to search for the best activities and methods for preschool children.

Patty Hill also regarded experimentation in the kindergarten department essential if the department were to maintain its status as part of a university and college which expected that theory would continually be subjected to scientific tests. In particular, she saw the need for new songs, stories, games, and materials that would maintain the child's attention without coercion from the teacher. Members of her department were able to test new ideas and materials at the Speyer and Horace Mann Schools, two experimental institutions run by Teachers College. They found, for example, that dolls were an excellent means of directing the child's play motive toward a problem which he must solve, because dolls had needs for which a child might spend days making things. In this revision of Froebel's occupations the teacher either proposed a project for the child and let him figure it out, or else helped the child work out something he himself proposed to do.

Patty Hill strongly advised her students to adopt a responsive rather than a tightly structured approach to each day's classroom work. She also warned them, however, about the pitfalls of trying to be too empirical. She divided teachers into two categories. The cookbook teacher, she said, "sits down in the evening, measures out so much arithmetic, so much spelling, so much music, according to a pedagogical recipe and next day spoon feeds it into his pupils. *He* calls the process education." The checkerboard teacher cannot operate that way. "Would it do any good to take the board the evening before and figure out the campaign—first this move, then that move? When he sat down with his opponents he would find that the vital factor had been entirely omitted from his calculations: the reaction of the other mind." While advocating use of all the current data and theories, Patty Hill appreciated some of the weakness of the child-study movement and urged her pupils: "Measure everything you can. But don't give up a thing simply because you can't measure it. We are only fumbling with these new tools. There are values that still escape our formulas." She thought that kindergartners had not received much real help from specialists in educational psychology in reconstructing the kindergarten program, and she criticized the fact that few psychological studies involved children under the age of six. Nevertheless, in her experimental approach to education, Hill obviously established herself in clear opposition to Susan Blow's description of sequence and procedure in the kindergarten.[24]

The courses offered in the kindergarten department at Teachers College also reflected the perspective of Patty Hill and Dean Russell. For example, Harriette Mills, teacher of the course on the kindergarten gifts and occupations, criticized the use of Froebel's original materials on several grounds. First, their small size created nervous agitation for the children using them; second, too much emphasis on their symbolic value relegated social aims of education to a back seat; and third, the traditional sequence in which those materials were used contradicted the child's mental growth, for the child need not develop logical thinking at that age. Mills argued instead that home and nature should be the main topics of the kindergarten curriculum, and the gifts and occupations should be subordinated to serve this subject matter. In addition she urged enlarging the gifts, removing the sequence, thus freeing the child from "bondage to form," and finally, introducing other kinds of materials such as dolls and bean bags. In another course, Kindergarten 13, Mary Runyan taught the neglected art of story telling. Her course presupposed a college-level background in English literature and in mythology. The students explored a broad spectrum of literature, not restricting themselves to the stories in Froebel's *Mutter und Köse Lieder*, and they discussed which selections were most appropriate for children and why.[25]

Susan Blow, to her grave disappointment, could not in fact turn back the tide of change at Teachers College. Writing Fanniebelle Curtis, she complained:

> I am finding it simply impossible to get the class at Teachers College to conceive Froebel's ideal because they nearly all have the idea that I am standing for a formal, arbitrary and unpsychologing [sic] procedure.[26]

Finally, after several years of lecturing there, Blow resigned, no longer desiring to work under Hill, with whom she disagreed so deeply. As she told Curtis: "I tried to convert and when conversion failed, left."[27] Dean Russell, delighted with the turn of events, recalled:

> Moral suasion had no effect upon advocates of a system handed down *ex cathedra* and dominated by the personality of Susan E. Blow. It is to the lasting credit of Patty Hill that she dared to meet the champion on her own grounds and in fair combat won the victory.[28]

Miss Blow may have despaired, but she did not give up hope. Even in the years following her defeat and resignation at Teachers College, while more and more kindergartners drifted into more experimental ways, Miss Blow retained her confidence. The kindergarten, she maintained, had principles and ideals more comprehensive than other educational practices and therefore could not and should not adjust itself to them. The opposite must occur. However, in holding that position she remained willing to accept the consequence that:

> . . . the conscious Froebelian cannot be popular. But if we are right we can forgo [sic] popularity. It is a great privilege to believe you have an insight which is slowly making a beneficent revolution.[29]

Some, like Lucy Wheelock, regarded the debate as healthy, bringing to the fore valuable discussion. Many of the "new" kindergarten ideas advocated by reformers, she said, were really a part of Froebel's original ideas, such as the emphasis on outdoor and nature activities. Froebel, of course, had had each child tend a garden, and he took children on walks and on fishing trips.

79

Thus despite the internal conflict within the kindergartners' movement there were important common principles. They agreed on self-activity or learning by doing; the encouragement of self-expression; the concept of growth in child development going from the simple to the complex; and the premise that education should concern the development of the whole child, spiritually, physically, and socially.[30] These factors alone represented a more unconventional attitude than most school teachers had at that time. Thus, as kindergartens became incorporated into many urban public school systems, all kindergartners, traditional or progressive, had new ideas to bring into the elementary school.

1. "Editorial," *The Century Magazine*, XIV (January 1893), 475. See also Mary D. Runyan, "The Training of Kindergartners," *Teachers College Record*, V (November 1904), 412; *New York Kindergarten Association Annual Report, 1903-1904*, 9.

2. John Dewey, *The School and Society* (Chicago: University of Chicago Press, 1956), 117-118, 132-138; Friedrich Froebel, *Education of Man* in Irene Lilley, *Friedrich Froebel* (Cambridge, England: Cambridge University Press, 1967), 66, 83.

3. G. Stanley Hall, "Some Defects of the Kindergarten in America," *Forum*, XXVIII (January 1900), 579-584; G. Stanley Hall, "Kindergarten Pedagogy," *Educational Problems* (New York: D. Appleton and Co., 1911), 11-13; Charles E. Strickland and Charles Burgess, editors, *Health, Heredity, and Growth: G. Stanley Hall on Natural Education* (New York: Teachers College Press, 1965), 18; Froebel, *Education of Man* in Lilley, 57, 58, 140.

4. G. Stanley Hall, "The Contents of Children's Minds on Entering School," *Pedagogical Seminary*, I (1891), 143-156; G. Stanley Hall, "Child Study: the Basis of Exact Education," *Forum*, XVI (December 1893), 429-441.

5. John Dewey, "The Kindergarten and Child Study," *National Educational Association Journal of Proceedings and Addresses* (1879), 586 (Hereinafter cited as *NEA*); Nina C. Vandewalker, "Relation of the Kindergarten to Child Study," *Kindergarten Review*, VIII (January 1898), 317-319; E. A. Kirkpatrick, "The Psychological Basis of the Kindergarten," *National Society for the Scientific Study of Education, Sixth Yearbook*, II (1907), 20-28 (Hereinafter cited as *NSSE*).

6. John Dewey, "A Pedagogical Experiment," *Kindergarten Magazine*, VIII (June 1896), 741. For a contemporary theory suggesting the observation of children's play as a device of psychoanalytic "child-study," see Erik Erikson, *Childhood and Society* (New York: Norton, 1964), 209-241.

7. Marguerite Bell, *With Banners: A Biography of Stella L. Wood* (St. Paul, Minnesota: Macalester College Press, 1954), 28-29; William N. Hailmann, "Opening Address," *NEA* (1887), 334; Patty Smith Hill, "The History of the Kindergarten Song in America," *Kindergarten-Primary Magazine*, XXIII (January 1911), 135-143; "Lucy Wheelock," *Dictionary of American Biography*, Supplement Four (New York: Charles Scribner's Sons, 1974), 874-875.

8. Edward L. Thorndike, "Notes on Psychology," *Teachers College Record*, IV (November 1903), 62; Dewey, *School and Society*, 119-120. See also Nina C. Vandewalker, "Relation of the Kindergarten to Child Study," *Kindergarten Review*, VIII (January 1898), 317-319; *Annual Report of the Silver Street Kindergarten Society, 1896*, 8-9; Richard G. Boone, "To the Michigan Kindergartners," *Kindergarten Magazine*, IX (January 1897), 363-370.

9. Patty S. Hill to William H. Burnham, New York City, October 28, 1931, printed in bound volume of letters entitled "To William H. Burnham, With Gratitude and Felicitation From Troops of Friends," Treasures Room, Clark University; Beulah Amidon, "Forty Years in Kindergarten: An Interview with Patty Smith Hill," *Survey Graphic*, XI (September 1927), 506-508.

10. Nora Atwood, "The Kindergarten and its Critics," *Kindergarten Magazine*, XVII (November 1904), 133-141; Edward L. Thorndike, "Notes on Psychology," *Teachers College Record*, IV (1903), 168-173; Laura Fisher, "The Kindergarten," *Report of the U.S. Commissioner of Education, 1903*, I, 719; Hall, *Educational Problems*, 27; Frederick Eby, "The Reconstruction of the Kindergarten," *The Pedagogical Seminary*, VII (1900), 229-286; Kirkpatrick, "The Psychologic Basis of the Kindergarten," 24-25.

11. Mary F. Schaefer, "Conservatism Versus Radicalism in the Kindergarten," *Education*, XXVII (September 1906), 37-44; M. V. O'Shea, "Current Criticism of the Kindergarten," *NEA* (1905), 365-370; Earl Barnes, "Symbolism in the Kindergarten," *NEA* (1893), 355-356.

12. Miss [Angeline] Brooks, "The Kindergarten Program," *Kindergarten Magazine*, VIII (January 1896), 343; Martha V. Collins, "The Kindergarten Materialist," *Kindergarten Magazine*, X (March 1898), 434-437.

13. Grace Owen, "A Study of the Original Kindergarten," *Elementary School Teacher*, VII (December 1906), 202-208.

14. Louisa Parsons Hopkins, "Education by Doing," *Kindergarten Magazine*, IV (November 1891), 171-173; A. S. Whitney, "Some Practical Results of Child Study," *Kindergarten Magazine*, VIII (April 1896), 539-545; "Editorial Notes," *Kindergarten Magazine*, VI (October 1893), 113.

15. Kate Douglas Wiggin, *My Garden of Memory: An Autobiography* (Boston: Houghton Mifflin Co., 1923), 132.

16. Susan Blow to Fanniebelle Curtis, September 9, 1910, Association of Childhood Education International Archives, Washington, D.C. (Hereinafter cited as ACEI).

17. Susan Blow to Fanniebelle Curtis, n.d., ACEI.

18. Jenny B. Merrill, "Methods of Child Study in the Kindergarten," *Kindergarten Magazine*, X (September 1897), 1-8; Laura Fisher, "Director's Report," *Report of the Boston School Committee, 1903*, 188-189; Stella Heinemann, "Public School Kindergartens in Milwaukee," *Kindergarten Magazine*, XVIII (April 1906), 460-462.

19. Sarah Stewart, "The International Kindergarten Union," *Kindergarten Magazine*, VI (September 1893), 1-8; International Kindergarten Union, *The Kindergarten* (Boston: Houghton Mifflin Co., 1913), ix-xiv (for a complete understanding of the different viewpoints, read published reports in this volume); Susan Blow to Fanniebelle Curtis, May 26, 1909, ACEI; Susan Blow to Fanniebelle Curtis, May 11, 1910, ACEI.

20. Lucy Wheelock, "The Changing and Permanent Elements in the Kindergarten," *Kindergarten Review*, XX (June, 1920), 603-611.

21. James Earl Russell, "The Kindergarten Outlook," *Teachers College Record*, V (November 1904), 408-411.

22. Amidon, "Forty Years in Kindergarten," 506-508, 523; "Patty Smith Hill," *Dictionary of American Biography*, Supplement Four (New York: Charles Scribner's Sons, 1974), 373-374.

23. Lawrence Cremin, *et al.*, *A History of Teachers College, Columbia University* (New York: Columbia University Press, 1954), 49-50; Patty S. Hill and Finnie Burton, "The Work of Anna E. Bryan in Louisville, Kentucky," *Kindergarten Magazine*, XIII (April 1901), 436-438; Amidon, "Forty Years in Kindergarten," 506; *New York Times*, May 26, 1946, 32:1; "Patty Smith Hill," *Dictionary of American Biography*, Supplement Four, 373-374.

24. Patty S. Hill, "The Future of the Kindergarten," *Teachers College Record*, X (November 1909), 37-38, 49-50; Hill, "Kindergartens of Yesterday and Tomorrow," *NEA* (1916), 294-295, 297; Hill, "Some Conservative and Progressive Phases of Kindergarten Education," *NSSSE Sixth Yearbook*, II (1907), 73.

25. Patty Smith Hill, "Introduction," *Teachers College Record*, XV (January 1914), 1-8.

26. Amidon, "Forty Years in the Kindergarten," 523; Hill, "Some Conservative and Progressive Phases," 69; Hill, "The Future of the Kindergarten," 49-50.

27. Harriette M. Mills, "The Kindergarten Gifts," *Teachers College Record*, V (November 1904), 83-85, 87-93; Mary D. Runyan, "Stories and Story-Telling for Kindergarten and Primary School," *Teachers College Record*, V (November 1904), 32-48; *Teachers College Announcement, 1902-1903*, Columbia University Bulletin of Information, 7.

28. Susan E. Blow to Fanniebelle Curtis, n.d., n.p., ACEI.

29. Susan E. Blow to Fanniebelle Curtis, n.d., n.p., ACEI.

30. James Earl Russell, *Founding Teachers College* (New York: Columbia University Press, 1937), 61.

31. Susan E. Blow to Fanniebelle Curtis, June 16, 1914, ACEI.

CHAPTER VI

KINDERGARTENS IN THE PUBLIC SCHOOLS

In hopes of making kindergartens available to all children, rich and poor alike, kindergarten organizations, allied with various women's groups, worked assiduously toward the establishment of kindergartens in public school systems. The general public knew something about the new enterprises as a result of publicity by charity kindergarten associations and exhibits at expositions and world's fairs in Philadelphia, St. Louis, Chicago, and the District of Columbia. Displays and speeches at National Educational Association conventions and pressure from local kindergarten associations had begun to make school administrators familiar with the idea. Although some kindergartners may have had qualms about whether the quality of their efforts would be maintained once sponsorship passed into the public schools, almost all of them engaged in strenuous efforts to achieve this aim. By 1914, they had achieved their goal in good measure, since every major city in the United States had municipal kindergartens. Success, however, both fulfilled and disappointed their expectations.

The arguments that were used to justify the support of kindergartens by public expenditure included many previously used for the establishment and support of charity endeavors. The President of the Baltimore Board of School Commissioners, for example, urged municipal kindergartens for those children whose parents could not rear them properly and who otherwise would be neglected and left to develop bad habits. The kindergarten in the public schools, he said, provided children with a "humanizing and enlightening" environment, and was thus one way of saving children from "chronic pauperism and crime." In 1902, William T. Harris reiterated his belief that the kindergarten was an excellent means of molding the child "weakling" produced by the urban slum. "As a matter of self-preservation," he wrote, "each city should organize a strong force of kindergartens throughout all precincts where the weaklings of society come together."[1]

Not all opinions were as baldly snobbish as Harris'. Sarah Cooper warned that society needed to concentrate on preventing rather than punishing crime. She insisted that children were not naturally depraved, but that they needed "wise care and training" to keep them from heading in the direction of evil. "The prevention of crime," she warned, was "the duty of society. Society has no right to punish crime at one end if it does nothing to prevent it at the other end." In view of that goal, she considered the public kindergarten an excellent means of setting young children on the road toward morally uplifted lives.[2] William Rainsford, pastor of St. George's Protestant Episcopal Church in New York City, also regarded public kindergartens as crucial in crowded urban areas where otherwise children imbibed evil and acquired vicious habits. In an article in the *Kindergarten Magazine* in 1895, one writer charged corrupt politicians with irresponsibility, especially those who filled their pockets with taxpayer's money or who spent millions of dollars on a "speedway" to be used only by city officials "to exercise their trotters," but who provided no money:

> to give our children sufficient room in the schools, to open kindergartens for those of tender age or to buy them fresh air, a plot of clean grass, a shade tree or a flower. It seems cheaper to those who govern us to let them grow up in filth, ignorance and vice and to swell the population of juvenile prisons and reformatories.[3]

For William T. Harris, industrial preparation provided "sufficient justification" for introducing kindergartens into the public school system. He said that if schools intended to prepare any children for arts and trades they had to start at the formative kindergarten age with the use of Froebel's gifts and occupations which developed skill and deftness of hand and accuracy of visual observation. Harris admitted that kindergartners considered this situation only incidental to the more important moral and intellectual nurture, but he himself regarded the kindergarten as providing a prerequisite for manual training which could then be continued in technical schools upon completion of the grades.[4]

In general, however, proposed benefits were not restricted to poor children. Arguments emphasized the importance of kindergartens for middle- and upper-class children as well. Sarah Cooper advised that all children should attend because the kindergarten insured "a happy, well-developed childhood, as the foundation-stone, laid deep down, on which may be reared a noble manhood and womanhood—the pride and glory of the State." Nicholas M. Butler, President of Columbia University, and others felt that kindergartens should be included in the public schools as a way for the current generation to prepare the next one: if the kindergarten had educational and moral validity then it should be available to all children, rich and poor together. They pointed out, for example, that in such preschool classes, children learned the meaning and responsibility of social relationships in several ways. A classroom with children of mixed ethnic backgrounds provided the pupils with effective lessons in heterogeneity and democracy. In their games and plays, the children enacted domestic or public roles, like being a parent or keeping a store, during which time they learned about civic and social associations. Many people also claimed that kindergartens mitigated the abrupt cultural shock for the young child entering primary school. Laura Fisher, director of Boston's public kindergartens, asserted that the preschool child became accustomed to being at school with playmates rather than at home with his family, to coming to school regularly and punctually, and to enjoying working both by himself and with others. With this background the child could then adapt quite easily to a good primary class where the teacher did not rely on fear and where the child could move freely, play, and sing.[5]

In the belief that kindergartens laid a physical, mental, and social foundation that would prepare children well for both their future school and adult lives, many influential people supported the idea of adding them to the public school system. In 1890, Andrew Draper, State Superintendent of Education in New York, claimed that a kindergarten experience made a child:

> more kindhearted, more in sympathy with nature, more in love with his or her fellow beings, a better citizen and a stronger man or woman at the age of twenty-one . . . than it is possible for the average child to be without this work.

85

As a consequence, he felt that if forced to make a choice, he would choose adoption of the kindergarten over the high school.[6] Six years later the long list of public kindergarten supporters included such personages as university presidents Charles W. Eliot of Harvard, Franklin Carter of Williams, Edward H. Griffin of Johns Hopkins, James Canfield of Ohio State, and David S. Jordan of Stanford. Canfield wrote that he would prefer seven grades with kindergarten over eight grades without it, and Jordan agreed with his Professor of Education Earl Barnes, who said that their "own university was founded on educational ideas and ideals, some of which were suggested to Mr. Stanford by his observation of kindergarten work."[7]

Nevertheless, supporters in the fight to establish municipal kindergartens frequently fought an uphill battle, especially when confronted with state laws determining the age that children might enter school. The significant problem was that although almost any city was permitted to maintain kindergartens with local funds, it could not receive state funds unless the legislature established provisions allowing children to enter school under the age of six. The New York and Illinois legislatures, for example, provided state funds for kindergartens on the same basis as for any other public school. However, in seven states, the state constitution, not ordinary legislation, determined the minimum school age, and change thus required a constitutional amendment. Missouri was such a case in point. In 1873, when the first public kindergarten opened in St. Louis under the direction of Susan Blow in the Des Peres School, the legal school age was set at five. Two years later, the Missouri State Legislature revised the constitution to read that legal school age started at six. Still, the St. Louis school board continued to admit five-year-olds until 1883 when a Missouri State Supreme Court decision declared the board's action illegal. The school board in conjunction with other interested parties tried repeatedly to change that provision, but without success. As late as 1912, the minimum school age remained at six. In the 1870's and early 1880's public kindergartens in St. Louis had flourished and provided a model for the nation because of the expert care of Blow and Harris. When they were prevented from accepting children under six years of age, however, the effectiveness of their program designed for children starting at ages three and four was hampered.[8]

Although Massachusetts had a state law for compulsory school attendance for children six through fourteen, it had no restriction whatever on the minimum age of school entry. Nor was provision for state funds a barrier, since in Massachusetts local taxes supported all public education. The difficulty lay in convincing the Boston School Committee and the City Council of the need to open public kindergartens. When Elizabeth Peabody failed in her attempts to convince them, Pauline Shaw stepped in in 1878 to provide privately paid training for kindergarten teachers and several free kindergartens. Many of the classes were housed in public school buildings, although Shaw paid for teachers' salaries and material expenses. In 1886, Shaw requested the School Committee to investigate the kindergartens with an eye toward adopting them as part of the regular school system. The investigating group reported that the kindergarten prepared a child for school and life better than most homes, even wealthy ones, and they recommended, therefore, that the City Council appropriate $20,000 in 1888 in support of public kindergartens. With the popularity of Pauline Shaw's kindergartens evident throughout the city, the City Council agreed handily to provide the funds, especially since many of them had been under the mistaken assumption all along that the city had paid the salaries and expenses for those kindergartens located in public school buildings. That year the *Annual Report of the Boston School Committee* jubilantly stated that the city had finally accepted the kindergartens, characterizing it as "the most noteworthy event of the year." Initially, the city supported nineteen kindergartens, including Shaw's fourteen, thirty-six teachers, and almost one thousand children. Superintendent Edwin P. Seaver wrote that he hoped to establish kindergartens staffed with exceptionally qualified teachers in every school in the city. The School Committee received requests from all over the city for kindergartens, and the number continued to multiply.[9]

In some cities, kindergartens entered the public schools through the strong influence and support of the school superintendent. In La Porte, Indiana, for example, Dr. William Hailmann introduced kindergartens into the public school system. A pioneer kindergarten advocate, Hailmann had published a kindergarten journal called *The New Education* which was later merged with Elizabeth Peabody's *Kindergarten Messenger* when these two leaders formed the American Froebel Union. The journal survived only a few years, but the zeal of Hailmann and his wife, Eudora, was permanent. Eudora Hailmann, well-versed in Froebel's ideas, opened new kindergartens, taught them, and ran a training class, while her husband, a nationally known progressive educator, advanced the kindergarten cause in his varying supervisory positions as head of the German-American Academy in Milwaukee, Superintendent of Schools in La Porte, and head of the United States Government Indian School in Washington.[10]

In most cities, however, as in the case of Boston, public kindergartens originated from efforts of private philanthropists. In 1892, the Chicago Board of Education voted to incorporate the ten privately sponsored kindergartens that had been operating in public school classrooms. Philadelphia appropriated funds in 1883 to help support the free kindergartens of the Sub-Primary School Society and four years later annexed all thirty of them. The Board of School Trustees of Richmond, Indiana, voted in 1889 to support the kindergartens which had opened two years earlier as a charity endeavor. In the early 1890's the Board of Education of Jamestown, New York, a small city south of Lake Chautauqua, and the Central Board of Education of Pittsburgh, Pennsylvania, took similar action. In 1901, the Free Kindergarten and Children's Aid Association of Pasadena, California, succeeded in having the City Charter revised to permit kindergartens in every school district. In 1893 Louisa Mann, daughter-in-law of Horace and Mary Mann, organized the Columbian Kindergarten Association to petition Congress to pass legislation bringing kindergartens into the public schools in the District of Columbia. This association, which had the active help of Phoebe Hearst and the daughter and wife of President Grover Cleveland, convinced Congress in 1898 to appropriate twelve thousand dollars for kindergartens for white and black children. The Cincinnati Kindergarten Association, while engaged in running free kindergartens, also devoted energy to making them part of the public schools. Interested parties travelled from Cincinnati to St. Louis to observe their system and to speak to Susan Blow and William T. Harris. Blow advised them strongly against paying the cost of an experimental kindergarten in the schools. She felt keenly that in order to succeed, experiments should be paid for by the school board from the very beginning.[11]

Kindergarten associations did not cease to function after a city's board of education provided for public kindergartens. They continued to work to make the kindergartens a realistic fulfillment, not a hollow promise. The New York Kindergarten Association remained active for more than forty years after the Board of Education voted in 1892 to authorize kindergartens in primary schools. Members of the association campaigned for support and increased allocation of funds, and they secured the endorsement of a long list of prominent New Yorkers: Hamilton Mabie, Mrs. Seth Low, Mr. and Mrs. Andrew Carnegie, Bayard Cutting, the Honorable Charles P. Daly, William C. Schermerhorn, Jacob H. Schiff, J. Pierpont Morgan, and Mrs. Cornelius Vanderbilt. On March 14, 1895, the Kindergarten Association held an open meeting for all businessmen at the Chamber of Commerce, and the speakers included Abram S. Hewitt, ex-mayor of New York City, and President Adolph L. Sanger of the School Board, who wished the association success in awakening widespread interest in kindergartens so that school authorities could justify allotting more tax money to kindergartens. In addition to the Kindergarten Association, other groups cooperated with the New York Board of Education. The Educational Alliance, for example, continued their own kindergartens and supported the city's through the donation of rooms in the Alliance Building.[12]

Later the National Kindergarten Association, organized in 1909 to promote public kindergartens, helped local associations carry on such campaigns. N.K.A. propagandizing activities included sending out circulars and letters, publishing journal and newspaper articles, producing a film called "At the Threshold of Life" with Thomas A. Edison, and lobbying for legislation pertinent to kindergartens. The N.K.A. coordinated its efforts with several organizations, such as the Chicago Kindergarten College, the International Kindergarten Union, the National Education Association, the General Federation of Women's Clubs, the National Congress of Mothers, and the National Council of Women. It joined forces with the California Congress of Mothers, for example, to petition the state legislature to pass a law in 1913 providing for the establishment and maintenance of public school kindergartens. At that time, only fourteen out of the fifty-eight counties in California had local public school kindergartens. A law finally passed that year allowing kindergartens to be established upon petition to local school boards by the parents of twenty-five children between the ages of four and six-and-a-half, living within one mile from an elementary school. Within two years, the efforts of the combined organizations succeeded in opening hundreds of new kindergartens.[13]

As in California, a school board decision or legislative action to permit kindergartens in the school system did not necessarily mean the opening of a kindergarten in every school. In New York City, for example, although legislation authorizing public kindergartens passed in 1892, the Superintendent of Schools did not report any rapid growth in the number of kindergartens until 1902. By that time, a significant change in the school law stated that any child entering school below six years of age could attend only kindergarten, not first grade. Second, the Board of Education began to supply more liberal funds for the establishment of kindergartens, and third, local school boards cooperated more fully in finding suitable premises. However, in New York City as elsewhere, lack of proper rooms and well-trained teachers still impeded progress.[14]

Nationally, the number of kindergartens in public schools spiralled in the years before World War I. According to the U.S. Commissioner of Education, by 1912 nine hundred cities had a total of 6,400 kindergartens with 312,000 children enrolled. These figures for public kindergartens accounted for about 85 per cent of all existing kindergartens and the pupils enrolled, with the remaining 15 per cent classified as "other than public," run by parochial schools, private schools, kindergarten associations, missions, settlements, mills, Government Indian Schools, and orphanages.[15]

Even though public kindergartens continually accommodated more children, the number attending was still only a small percentage of the total population of four to six year olds. For example, in 1912, five states had less than 1 per cent of this age group enrolled; fifteen states had 1 percent to 3 per cent; eight states had 3 per cent to 5 per cent; eight more states had 5 per cent to 10 per cent; and five states had 10 per cent to 15 per cent. Colorado and Michigan had 15 per cent to 20 per cent, Wisconsin, New York, and Connecticut had 20 per cent to 25 per cent, and New Jersey, District of Columbia, and Rhode Island had 25 percent to 30 per cent. In terms of concrete numbers this meant, for example, that for every one thousand children between the ages of four and six in New Jersey, 278 were enrolled in kindergarten.[16]

Despite some negative reaction, schools seemed to evaluate their kindergartens in essentially positive terms, as letters from primary teachers, supervisors, and school superintendents bore out some of the numerous claims for the kindergarten. Agnes Manning, a public school teacher in California, wrote to Superintendent John Swett saying that she always knew which children came to her from the kindergarten, for they were more observant, honest, attentive, and verbal, and gentler spoken. In 1914, the United States Bureau of Education received one hundred letters from primary teachers in Boston stating their confidence in kindergarten training as a good foundation for the primary teacher to build upon. For example, teachers said the songs and excursions extended the child's knowledge of the world and encouraged his curiosity; the handwork made it easier for him to learn to use a pen and to write; the work and play with the gifts, Froebelian educational materials, awakened his notion of number; while the stories sparked his interest in and desire for good poetry and prose. A typical comprehensive statement of the benefits a child derived from a kindergarten program came from Jane A. Hind, a primary teacher from P.S. No. 26 in Manhattan, who wrote that children coming from the kindergarten were:

> more intelligent, quicker in their movements, more studious in their habits, more nimble with their fingers, and gentle towards each other. They seem to be happy in their work and very often connect their lessons with those they learned while in the kindergarten . . . , while those who have not been in kindergarten seem to be slower in comprehending the work that is put before them.[17]

Opinions from primary supervisors and principals collected by the Bureau of Education indicated whole-hearted approval from most of them. Constance Mackenzie, a supervisor of public kindergartens in Philadelphia, reported in 1895 that initial opposition gave way as the better primary school teachers changed their attitudes and recognized the less tangible aspects of a good kindergarten. W. M. Fosdick, a principal in San Diego, said that his teachers unanimously approved of the kindergartens both for reasons already mentioned and because of the "happier outlook upon school life" which children gained through their kindergarten experience. Lucy Bristol, a supervisor in Louisville, and Ella Boyce, from Pittsburgh, felt that all children should be required to attend kindergarten. School superintendents generally expressed enthusiasm about kindergartens in their systems. C. Edward Jones of Albany, New York, for example, stated that kindergartens there had operated for many years so successfully that "we would hardly know how to maintain a public-school system without them." Superintendent F. H. Bede, in New Haven, Connecticut, where there had been public kindergartens since 1892, observed in 1912 that primary teachers had become more appreciative of kindergartens during the past fifteen years as they themselves became more progressive. Earlier they had disapproved of them because they felt the children were not obedient or formal enough. Every "up-to-date" first grade teacher preferred kindergarten children, he said, while the old-fashioned teacher, interested primarily in discipline, still disapproved.[18]

Several surveys besides those of individual superintendents and the U.S. Bureau of Education tried to give insight into the effects of kindergarten training. In 1905, Francis Holden surveyed the opinions of six thousand teachers across the country. His replies indicated total agreement with the statement that the kindergarten was an "excellent preparation for the studies taught in the primary schools," although individual reasons varied. Other studies tried to show that children with kindergarten training repeated grades less frequently than others, that they progressed faster or slower, or that they learned to read faster. Unfortunately, their weak experimental design made the findings of these studies unreliable.[19]

Once in the school system, however, kindergartens became subjected to new pressures and changes. For example, they were usually assigned to undesirable rooms. Several school surveys heavily criticized the conditions of the kindergartens for a lack of hygienic conditions, insufficient space, or improper furniture. They also indicated that the fault usually lay with school administrators who relegated kindergartens to rooms that no one else wanted. Such rooms usually lacked closet space for materials, a bright, sunny exposure, proper ventilation, and child-size toilet facilities.[20]

Kindergartners also faced a problem with administrators who frequently expected them to teach both a morning and an afternoon session. Administrators argued that: (1) elementary school teachers taught all day and so should kindergartners; (2) twice as many children could be accommodated; and (3) it wasted public funds to leave the kindergarten room empty half the day. Initially, all kindergartners seemed to object to two sessions. Primarily, they felt that they needed their afternoons for home visitation, holding mothers' meetings, and attending classes for their own educational improvement. The double session eliminated most of those activities if only for lack of time. Also, kindergartners pointed out that a single session might only last three hours, but the teacher expended a great deal of energy during that time being alert, patient, and innovative.

Most agreed that even the best kindergartner was not equal to a second session with a new group of children and that afternoon classes were too harried and rushed. In addition, they said that not only the teacher, but the preschool child could not profitably sustain his concentration for the afternoon. If both sessions were to consist of the same children, the argument ran, the children could not keep going all day long in directed activities; and if it were different children each time, the afternoon children would be too tired from having played at home since early morning. Finally, double session opponents recommended that in the afternoons the kindergarten room could be used as a play center or an extra room for the over-crowded primary grades.[21]

Yet double sessions became increasingly common, and some kindergartners rationalized that accommodating more children along with the possibility of smaller classes would make the ad-vantages outweigh the disadvantages. By 1912, over two thirds of the almost nine hundred cities with public kindergartens had double sessions.[22]

The most significant change brought about by double sessions was the declining involvement of kindergartners in community affairs and the crippling of their social work functions. While everyone continued to consider the ideal kindergartner a social worker as well as a teacher, the ideal rang hollow when the kindergartner had to work in school each afternoon. In that case, she had only enough time to plan the next day's classes and hold an occasional mothers' meeting, but she lacked the time for intimate home contact. If she did make a visit, it usually had to be at the busiest time of the afternoon when mothers were preparing dinners and older chil-dren were home from school.

Kindergartners continued to emphasize the importance of home visiting in creating a closer relationship between home and school,[23] but only in a few cities like Brooklyn, Cincinnati, and Boston, where the kindergartner had the time to devote to such activities, did home visiting remain a reality. In Brooklyn and Queens, for example, there were almost three hundred kindergartens in 1905, and their teachers made a total of 4,445 home visits.[24] A few years earlier Boston kindergarten supervisor Laura Fisher reported that visitation formed a vital part of their program, and that teachers performed this duty "faithfully and enthusiastically."[25] In Cincinnati, the kin-dergartners broke up their afternoon work among several activities.

One day a week they attended conferences run by the Cincinnati Kindergarten Association. Two days they directed primary children in kindergarten activities in the kindergarten room for an hour. The rest of their afternoon time they spent in home visitation, during 1911-1912 making a total of over nine thousand visits to the homes of 2,833 children.[26] In other cities most kindergartners in public schools did hold mothers' or parents' meetings, usually monthly, to get acquainted with the families, to explain the meaning of the kindergarten work, and to enlist their interest. These meetings, however, could not replace the knowledge gained about a child and the help the kindergartner could offer the mother during more relaxed home visits in cities when she had the opportunity.

Another pressure that brought change was the school's concern that the kindergarten equip the child for success in the primary grades. While campaigning for public kindergartens, advocates had urged them as a valuable preparation for life and school, but after their legal adoption, the debate over their value narrowed to the latter concern. Clearly some teachers found kindergartens unsatisfactory preparation, regarding kindergarten children in need of stricter discipline. Alida Conover, a teacher from Bayonne, New Jersey, for example, felt the children in her first grade class who came from the kindergarten were "more restless, less attentive, less interested in primary work, and showed less application than those who entered the grades directly." She also found the kindergarten children more difficult to discipline, since, she said, they were used to chattering, and moving about freely. A teacher from Jamestown, New York, suggested that children spend their last semester in the kindergarten working in complete silence in order to prepare for first grade. In New York City, replies from principals and primary teachers regarding kindergarten included several who objected to the children's naturalness and called it lack of discipline. Superintendent D. J. Kelly of Binghamton, New York, insisted that the kindergarten only had value when it directly and specifically prepared a child for the first grade, and he urged kindergartners to work on producing in their pupils "the same degree of uniformity as any product of the school."[27]

In 1899, a scathing article written by Marion Carter, a primary school teacher, appeared in the *Atlantic Monthly*. The author, describing and generalizing her own opinions, said that she and other primary teachers had looked forward to a "pedagogical millennium" as the first group of kindergarten children came to the grades, but that instead, they found only disappointment. Carter cited several reasons for their dismay. The children paid no attention unless their interests were being catered to or unless they were being entertained, and they did not enjoy traditional instruction in the three r's. In one instance, she related, a kindergarten teacher had built a model volcano for the children to explain the phenomena of the explosion: she cut a rubber ball in half, filled it with alcohol-soaked cotton, put it beneath sand, and lit it. Carter registered her exasperation with the fact that those children then expected similar experiences in the first grade. Moreover, the children failed to follow directions exactly. When asked to draw an apple, for example, one child drew a little boy picking apples from a tree. Finally, Carter objected to the kind of nature work done in some kindergartens. If she handed out three leaves and asked the children what they had on their desks, the answers came back as three little boats, three fans, or a mama, papa, and baby. The kindergartner may have claimed to have trained the children's imaginations, but according to Carter she had trained only their "suggestability" and in so doing had injured their ability to think clearly and concretely. Claiming to speak for primary school teachers, Carter concluded that their "abilities were not such as to enable . . . them successfully to develop in the primary school the flabby kindergarten intellect of the kindergarten child."[28]

Some kindergartners, of course, defended themselves against such attacks, but others succumbed to the pressures. Responding to complaints about discipline problems, one kindergartner wrote that in most instances the first grade teacher was probably as much at fault as the child or kindergartner. Similarly, Alice Putnam explained that trouble would inevitably arise when elementary school teachers used conventional methods to instruct children from a kindergarten, without understanding or building upon their former experiences. Such children, she said, were used to combining mental, physical, and moral training with a variety of activities, whereas teachers in primary grades often tried to make children sit silently for a whole day without exercises and activities. Nicholas Murray Butler insisted that teachers who complained about the lack of discipline among kindergarten children misunderstood the true concept of discipline. For example, he said, an observer passing over New York City in a balloon would see a jumble of people moving disorderly in all directions, not in a military-like formation. Upon closer observation, however, he would see each person going about his own business without disturbing anyone about him. In sum, he said he preferred "to see more of the kindergarten order in the lower grades of the elementary school and less of the elementary school order in the kindergarten." Despite such support, the demand for the kindergarten to subordinate its goals to those of the school often led to what Patty Hill called "the tyranny of the primary teacher." She complained that it frequently caused kindergartners to sacrifice their ideals in exchange for the approval that came from well-disciplined and well-scrubbed children who did neat, accurate manual work.[29]

However, if the kindergarten lost some of its old identity and function in the public school, it also helped to revamp the primary school program in the process of coordinating the kindergarten methods and goals with those of the primary grades. In the course of cooperating in order to reduce the gap the child faced in transition from preschool classes to first grade, the kindergarten did offer some resistance to being molded and swallowed up by the public school institution, and in so doing contributed to changing primary teaching. In fact, a leading kindergartner at the beginning of the twentieth century felt that the transformation of primary education that had occurred was largely due to the kindergarten influence, and that it was a fact "so thoroughly recognized as to need but passing mention."[30]

Cities and schools tried various ways of achieving a more unified kindergarten-primary program, but one common theme prevailed: primary and kindergarten teachers should be very familiar with one another's work. This took several forms, such as: visiting each other's classroom; taking courses in each other's field; both receiving the same normal training as a unified course; the kindergartner spending afternoons in a primary classroom or with primary children playing in the kindergarten room; and both teachers coordinating their lesson plans and units in order to build upon and take advantage of what the children already knew. The kindergarten supervisor in Louisville, Mary D. Hill, explained that in their schools, kindergarten and primary teachers together devised a list of ten stories, ten poems, songs, handcrafts, and other skills and habits which every kindergartner should use or teach to her children. The primary teacher then planned her lessons, building on the material already familiar to the children. In Kalamazoo, Michigan, where in 1914 almost all the children attended kindergarten, an exemplary cooperation was reported between teachers, and hiring practices gave preferences to primary teachers with kindergarten training.[31]

Lucy Wheelock, kindergarten leader and teacher of a kindergarten training class, saw the relationship between the kindergartner and primary teacher as requiring "mutual acquaintance and sympathy." The particular materials used were unimportant if the goal in both kindergarten and primary was to lead to "the more perfect unfolding of the human being."[32] Since she believed that the child develops gradually and continually, she considered it significant to avoid any gap between kindergarten and primary work. Thus, as Lucy Wheelock's kindergarten training class grew into a school, her future teachers were trained in kindergarten, primary, and later, nursery school education.

In terms of actual classroom procedure and curriculum, the primary grades incorporated much from the kindergarten. While many of these practices may have been recommended, more clearly defined, and extended by progressive educators, they were clearly a part of the earlier kindergarten program. For example, the customary discipline of rigid stillness and obedience gave way in numerous grade school classes to a gentler approach and a spirit of cooperation. In 1893, St. Paul, Minnesota's Superintendent of Schools Charles B. Gilbert wrote that kindergartens not only benefited the children attending them but that: "their spirit pervaded the school system. The discipline [was] gentler and more wholesome." He also felt that teachers gave more of their "attention to the moral and intellectual improvement of the child and less to technicalities and arbitrary rules."[33]

In addition, a growing number of primary teachers used or adapted kindergarten songs, games, and physical exercise in their classes. In 1889, Superintendent Edwin P. Seaver of Boston criticized the "present tendency" of the primary grades "to words, words, words; reading, forever reading," and he urged them to rectify the situation by using Froebel's more advanced activities.[34] In 1899, the *Kindergarten Magazine* published some letters from Boston first grade teachers reporting if and how they carried on kindergarten activities in their classes. One teacher, Louise Robinson, regretted that her syllabus allowed only twelve minutes a day for exercise, divided into three four-minute periods. Required to spend

97

the morning period on calisthenics, she then stretched the afternoon break to ten minutes, at which time the children played traditional kindergarten games. Showing us how slowly the notion of the educative value of play penetrated school procedure, Robinson closed her letter saying that her schedule meant:

> nearly an hour a week devoted to mere play. Is it worthwhile? I wish it were two hours a week as I think of the pleasure and profit derived from our playtime.[35]

Another teacher wrote saying that she used some songs and games in connection with lessons, continued a few of the occupations like peg work, stick laying, cutting, and color work, held morning talks, and took the children on excursions to nearby fields. She pointed out that these were such integral parts of their primary program that "we sometimes forget that they are a continuation of the kindergarten and came to us through its influence."[36]

Teachers in primary schools also came to recognize the value of the traditional kindergarten emphasis on children "learning by doing," that is, through activities that appealed to their interests, through discovery, and through agencies "other than the alphabet and multiplication table." The kindergartner suggested to the primary teacher that the child, not the subject, needed to be taught, that the emphasis in education should have been in arousing the child's natural development and abilities, and that "the road to knowledge for the child need not be steep and thorny."[37] Likewise, Colonel Francis Parker predicted that the primary grades would profit from fewer spelling books, less grammar, less arithmetic, and "more of the light of nature of the sort that Froebel meant should come into the kindergarten and school room."[38]

In the area of art education, too, the kindergarten contributed heavily to changing the primary school program. Schools had started introducing drawing for purely commercial reasons in the mid-nineteenth century, and this trend continued in the form of manual training schools. But with the influence of kindergartens and progressive primary educators, art education changed to a more aesthetic and expressive activity for the child. Primary schools came to realize and appreciate the fact that a child's art work, even if crude to the adult, expressed that child's world and, as such, should be valued. Many schools expanded their concepts of art education in the early 1890's by introducing the newly-designed Prang Art

98

Course in which children drew scenes of history, literature, or any other subject from their imaginations instead of by imitation. This course postponed emphasis on technique and verisimilitude for more advanced grades.[39]

Another form of art education popular in the United States in the 1890's was the Swedish Slöyd system, designed to teach children to build and make simple objects as a means of harmonizing the physical, moral, and mental aspects of a child's development. Cygaenus, the originator of the Slöyd system, acknowledged his debt to Froebel in the conception of his ideas, but expanded his own activities to include such things as wood working, all kinds of paper, crayons, and paint. Also, unlike most manual training which aimed mainly at mechanical skill in using tools, the Slöyd program emphasized the construction of forms and complete models. Very popular in elementary schools, Slöyd proved to be a connecting link between the kindergarten and manual training.[40]

The traditional holding of mothers' meetings also awakened the school's interest in community involvement. Increasingly, primary teachers began to hold mothers' meeting of their own, sometimes together with the kindergartners.[41] Although the school usually did not achieve the degree of neighborhood concern that the kindergarten had, it did develop interest in closer ties with the home. The kindergartner's meetings with parents involving them in their children's education were forerunners of the modern Parent Teacher Associations found in most school districts in the United States today.

Thus, the kindergarten movement in this country, which began as an agent of social and educational reform, succeeded in its goal of establishing kindergartens in the public schools. This resulted both in opening an opportunity for greater numbers of children to attend kindergartens than private associations could have accommodated and in helping to change the educational approach in the primary grades; however, it also led to a modification of the kindergarten's functions. Double sessions and an increasing emphasis on coordinating the programs of the preschool and first few grades brought about a corresponding stress on the child in school, rather than on the child in his total environment, that is, his home, his family, and his neighborhood. No longer did kindergarten teachers establish direct contact with their pupils' families; no longer did they work directly to close the gap between the immigrant or rural parents and their

99

Americanized or urban child. In short, kindergartners lost much of their opportunity to express their humane concern for social welfare that had characterized the free kindergartens of the late nineteenth century.

1. *Report of the School Commissioners of Public Schools of Baltimore, 1884,* xxxii-xxxiii, *1898,* 62-63, and *1899,* 50-51, 102-105; William T. Harris, "The Kindergarten as a Preparation for the Highest Civilization," *Kindergarten Magazine,* XV (June 1903), 615.

2. Sarah B. Cooper, "The Organic Union of Kindergarten and Primary School," *National Educational Association Journal of Addresses and Proceedings* (1893), 340 (Hereinafter cited as *NEA*); "Why Should the Kindergarten be Municipalized?" *Kindergarten Magazine,* IX (March 1897), 5-7.

3. Augusta Larned, "Public School Lambs," *Kindergarten Magazine,* VII (January 1895), 774.

4. William T. Harris, "Superintendent's Report," *Annual Report of the St. Louis Public Schools, 1879-1880,* 126-142; William T. Harris, "The Kindergarten in the Public School System," *Journal of Education,* XXXI (December 1881), 625-642.

5. Sarah B. Cooper, "Shall the Kindergarten be a Part of the Public School System of the State," MS lecture, Sarah Cooper Papers, Cornell University Regional Archives, Ithaca, New York; *New York Times,* April 2, 1880, 8:6; Nicholas Murray Butler, "Some Criticisms of the Kindergarten," *Educational Review,* XVIII (October 1899), 290; see published letter from Elizabeth Harrison to Education Commission, Chicago, October 5, 1898, in *Report of the Educational Commission of Chicago* (Chicago, 1899), 192-193; Laura Fisher, "Director's Report," *Report of the School Committee of Boston, 1897,* 169-170. See also William T. Harris, "Kindergarten and the Primary School," *NEA* (1891), 531.

6. *Report of the United States Commissioner of Education, 1890-1891,* 1046.

7. "Why Should the Kindergarten by Municipalized?" 501-516.

8. Frank Fitzpatrick, "What Shall the State do Toward the Education of Children Below the School Age?" *NEA* (1892), 628; *Report of the U.S. Commissioner of Education, 1897-1898,* 2539-2541; *Annual Report of the Board of Education of St. Louis, 1898-1899,* 55-56; "Editorial," *Educational Review,* VII (February 1894), 207-208.

9. "Superintendent's Report," *Annual Report of the School Committee of Boston, 1887,* 28-32, and *1889,* 14-17; *Annual Report of the School Committee of Boston, 1887,* 18-22, *1888,* 10-13, *1889,* 14-15, *1890,* 14-15; Edwin P. Seaver, "Discussion," *NEA* (1892), 638-640.

10. Barbara Greenwood, "William Nicholas Hailmann," in International Kindergarten Union, *Pioneers* (New York: The Century Co., 1924), 245-262; Charles H. Doerflinger, "The Kindergarten Movement in Milwaukee," *Kindergarten Magazine,* XVIII (March 1906), 385-406.

11. Laura Fisher, "The Kindergarten," *Report of the U.S. Commissioner of Education, 1903,* vol. I, 702; Alice Temple, *Survey of the Kindergarten of Richmond, Indiana* (Chicago: The University of Chicago Press, 1917), 2; Cora E. Harris, "Kindergarten Movement in Jamestown, New York," *Kindergarten Magazine,*

XII (February 1900), 305-308; Caroline H. McCulloch, "The Pittsburgh and Allegheny Free Kindergarten Association," *Kindergarten Magazine*, VII (April 1895), 596-597; *Pasadena Kindergartens, 1901-1919*, 10-11; Nina Vandewalker, *Kindergartens in American Education* (New York: The Macmillan Co., 1923), 70; Editors, "Public Kindergartens in Washington," *Educational Review*, XVI (September 1898), 208; Susan Blow to Benedict Excelsior, St. Louis, August 7, 1879, Taft Family Papers, Library of Congress, Washington, D.C.

12. "Editorial Notes," *Kindergarten Magazine*, V (September, 1892), 61; *New York Times* (March 13, 1895), 9:4, (March 15, 1895), 16:1 and (March 17, 1895), 16:4; *Annual Report of the Educational Alliance, 1898*, 38, *1899*, 16, and *1900*, 47-48.

13. *Report of the National Kindergarten Association, 1909-1911*, 3-5, 27-28; Lillian M. Clark, "Kindergarten Legislation in California," *NEA* (1915), 632-637; Mrs. H. N. Rowell, "What the California Congress of Mothers has Done for Kindergarten Legislation," *NEA* (1915), 631.

14. *Fourth Annual Report of [New York] City Superintendent of Schools, 1902*, 41-42, 92.

15. All figures over 500 are rounded off to the nearest hundred. For precise data, see *Kindergartens in the United States* (U.S. Bureau of Education Bulletin, no. 6, 1914), 16-17 53-85. In addition, several hundred kindergartens failed to return any data, *ibid.*, 86-92.

16. *Ibid.*, 7, 12, 15.

17. *Annual Report of [New York] City Superintendent of Schools, 1899*, 265: published letter from Miss Agnes Manning to Superintendent Swett in Sarah B. Cooper, "The Organic Union of Kindergarten and Primary School," *NEA* (1893), 341; *Kindergartens in the U.S.*, 108-113.

18. "Kindergarten History," *Kindergarten Magazine*, VIII (December 1895), 282; and *Kindergartens in the U.S.*, 96-97, 99, 104-106.

19. Francis Cooke Holden, "Does Kindergarten Training Prepare the Child for the Primary School?—The Teacher's Point of View," *Kindergarten Magazine*, XVII (March, 1905), 389-396. For other studies see Ernest O. L. Holland, "The Effect of Kindergarten Work on Children in the Grades," *NEA* (1913), 452-458: Martha MacLear, "A Study of the Work Done by Kindergarten Children in the First Grade," *Educational Review* (May 1914), 512-517; Willis L. Gard, "The Influence of Kindergarten on Achievement in Reading," *Educational Research Bulletin*, III (April 2, 1924), 135-138.

20. Waite, 2, and *Report of the Survey of the Public School System of Baltimore, Maryland, 1920-1921*, 148-150.

21. Fanniebelle Curtis and Constance MacKenzie Durham, "Normal Training Exchange," *Kindergarten Magazine*, XII (January 1900), 275-281; published letter from Mary M. Blodgett to Chicago Educational Commission, July 13, 1898, Chicago, in *Report of the Educational Commission of Chicago*, 96; Fisher, "The Kindergarten," 704.

22. For a more detailed description, see Luella A. Palmer, *Adjustment Between Kindergarten and First Grade* (U.S. Bureau of Education Bulletin, no.24, 1915), 25, 28-31; *Kindergartens in the U.S.*, 19-52.

23. U.S. Bureau of Education, *Organizing Kindergartens in City School Systems* (Kindergarten Education Circular, no. 2 revised, 1923): U.S. Bureau of Education, *The Kindergarten and Americanization* (Kindergarten Circular, no. 3, November 1918): Jenny B. Merrill, "Report of the Kindergartens: Boroughs of Manhattan, The Bronx, and Richmond," *Eighth Annual Report of the [New York] City Superintendent of Schools, 1906*, 301-304.

24. Fanniebelle Curtis, "Report of Kindergartens: Boroughs of Brooklyn and Queens," *Eighth Annual Report of the [New York] City Superintendent of Schools, 1906*, 305-306. See also, Fanniebelle Curtis, "Mothers' Meetings in Public School Kindergartens," *Kindergarten Magazine*, XII (November 1899), 161.

25. Fisher, "Kindergarten Director's Report," *Report of the Boston School Committee, 1895*, 269.

26. Julia S. Bothwell, "Kindergarten," *Cincinnati Public Schools Annual Report, 1911-1912*, 77-81; I. F. B. Dyer, "The Place of the Kindergarten in the Public School," *NEA* (1909), 439-440.

27. *Kindergartens in the U.S.*, 111-112, 98; "Opinions of Principals and First Year Teachers With Regard to the Work of the Kindergarten," *First Annual Report of the [New York] City Superintendent of Schools, 1899*, 267.

28. Marion Hamilton Carter, "The Kindergarten Child—After the Kindergarten," *Atlantic Monthly*, LXXXIII (March 1899), 358-366.

29. Edna Prather, "Kindergarten Discipline," *Kindergarten Magazine*, VIII (January 1896), 365-368; Alice Putnam, "The Use of Kindergarten Material in Primary Schools," in Four Active Workers, *The Kindergarten and the School* (Springfield: M. Bradley Co., 1886), 102-103; Butler, "Some Criticisms of the Kindergarten," 290-291; Patty S. Hill, "The Future of the Kindergarten," *Teachers College Record*, X (November 1900), 48. See also J. L. Meriam, "Practical Means of Unifying the Work of the Kindergarten and the Primary Grades," *NEA* (1916), 433-434.

30. *Kindergartens in the U.S.*, 10-11; Nina C. Vandewalker, "The History of the Kindergarten Influence in Elementary Education," *National Society for the Scientific Study of Education* (NSSSE) *Sixth Yearbook*, II (1907), 115. See also Ada Van Stone Harris, "Introduction," *NSSSE* (1907), 10.

31. Mary D. Hill, "The Educational Values Which the Child Carries Over From the Kindergarten Into the Primary Grades," *NEA* (1916), 430-432; *Kindergartens in the U.S.*, 108, 19-53; Waite, 15, 39; and Fisher, "The Kindergarten," 705.

32. Lucy Wheelock, "From the Kindergarten to the Primary School," *Childhood Education*, XVIII (May, 1942), 414-416. Wheelock recalled that she originally gave this paper as a lecture in Chicago in 1894.

33. "Editorial," *Educational Review*, VII (February 1894), 207. See also *Report of the U.S. Commissioner of Education, 1880*, ciii; James L. Hughes, "The Relation of the Kindergarten to the Public School System," *Kindergarten Magazine*, VI (June-July 1894), 756-757; Francis E. Cook, "The Kindergarten as an Educational Force," *Kindergarten Magazine*, XII (February 1900), 315-327.

34. "Superintendent's Report," *Report of the School Committee of Boston, 1889*, 18. See also Jenny Merrill, "Report of the Supervisor of Kindergartens in New York City," *Kindergarten Magazine*, XI (October 1898), 105-110; Nina Vandewalker "The History of the Kindergarten Influence in Elementary Education," 120-121.

35. "Normal Training Exchange," *Kindergarten Magazine*, XI (March 1899), 447-449.

36. *Ibid.*, 450-451.

37. Charles McKenny, "The Contributions of the Kindergarten to Elementary Education," *Kindergarten-Primary Magazine*, XXI (November 1908), 37-41; Irwin Shepard, "The Effects of the Kindergarten Training on the Primary School," *NEA* (1890), 559. See also Louise Pollock, "Kindergarten Methods in Primary

Schools," *American Journal of Education*, XXXI (1881), 643-650; Vandewalker, "History of the Kindergarten Influence," 120.

38. Francis W. Parker, "The Child," *NEA* (1889), 481.

39. Mary D. Hicks, "Prang Course of Art Instruction in Public Education," *Kindergarten Magazine*, V (September 1892), 40-47.

40. Gustave Larson, "Slöyd and Manual Training Contrasted," *Kindergarten Magazine*, III (October 1893), 92-98; Lawrence Cremin, *The Transformation of the School* (New York, 1961), 33; Olive Russell and Alice O'Grady, *Gateways to Art and Industry* (Springfield: M. Bradley Co., 1913) 1-10; Alice B. Stockham, "Slöyd in St. Paul," *The Kindergarten*, III (September 1890), 21-22.

41. Vandewalker, *Kindergarten in American Education*, 53-54; Palmer, 14; Marguerite Bell, *With Banners* (St. Paul, Minnesota: Macalester College Press, 1954), 56-57; Fisher, "Director's Report," *1903*, 190.

SUMMARY

The kindergartners had deep and lasting effects on American education because they concentrated with unflagging energies on problems which later became—and remain to this day—gut issues of education in a democratic society. Issues such as the relationship of teachers, parents, and children; whether the goals of the kindergarten should be to prepare children for the primary grades or whether the emphasis should be on the social and creative development of the child; and whether the role of school should be to help poor children achieve social mobility. These problems are still being argued by eminent educators, psychiatrists, psychologists, philosophers, sociologists, and politicians today.

Kindergartners understood better than anyone the need for relationships with parents and were eminently successful in these relationships. This work was interrupted by the introduction of kindergartens to the public school systems, where short sighted school administrators gradually eliminated kindergartners' home visits for financial reasons. The kindergartners, however, continued to involve parents, despite the hampering of their efforts, and to influence administrators and grade school teachers to appreciate the importance of contact with the home and with such organizations as the Congress of Parents and Teachers. Educators continue these efforts today. For example, in 1964 the Western New York Kindergarten Planning Committee issued a policy statement on the significance of cooperation between parents, teachers, and administrators. The suggestions clearly recall the goals of the early kindergartners, such as inviting mothers and fathers to evening meetings to better understand their children and the goals of the kindergarten, encouraging

104

teachers to make home visits, and inviting parents to observe a kindergarten in operation.[1] Among the numerous programs which now involve parents in early childhood education today are the Saturday School for Mothers and Preschoolers in Washington, D.C., and the Ford Foundation Pre-School Enrichment Program for disadvantaged children.[2]

The early kindergartners objected strongly to teaching reading in their classes, a problem that they anticipated and feared at the same time that they were lobbying to get kindergartens into the public schools. Their ambivalence was overcome by their recognition of the need to reach as many children as possible, something which they felt only public financing could accomplish. This question of teaching reading is still debated today, since there are still those who discuss the kindergarten in terms of its contribution to reading and academic development in the face of evidence to the contrary. Research has indicated no significant differences between programs using reading readiness workbooks and programs using normal kindergarten play activities. Such leading experts in teaching reading as Nila Banton Smith and George D. Spache have stated that formal reading readiness is contraindicated in the kindergarten, and that the kindergarten should be the place for the child to have formal language experiences,[3] a position reminiscent of the original Froebelians. The problem continues to plague the kindergartens.

While the pioneer kindergartners recognized that all children, regardless of background, could profit from attending kindergarten, they hoped to give poor children the opportunity to enrich their lives and give them some of the experiences that would enhance their social and intellectual growth. Seventy years later, Operation Headstart emerged with much the same goal, emphasizing compensatory experiences for both social and academic readiness.[4] The kindergartners were optimistic about the salutory effects of compensatory education, but they were not blind to the problems that existed. They hoped that the principles they introduced in early childhood education would serve as a basis for a reform in the entire elementary school system. Contemporary educators recognize early childhood education as part of a continuum which represents the process of learning and have in recent years urged that gains made in pre-school programs be reinforced in primary grades. While the kindergartners had hoped to have a stronger influence on the elementary school, they nevertheless left a visible imprint and provided kinder-

105

garten children with a strong foundation for their future development.

In summary, it is clear that these dedicated, enlightened women set their sights on educational needs that have continued to beset society to our own day. In their work, they set models and identified problems with which we are still grappling. Perhaps it was their idealism as well as their dedication, intelligence, and zeal that after all has the greatest relevance for us today. This ideal is embodied in Lucy Wheelock's plea to kindergartners in 1924 to maintain their ideals as well as their ideas:

> We need the bard, the minstrel and the story-teller today. The soul of music is not dead. It lives in every child's heart and should voice itself in a child's song. The teacher should 'lend to the rhyme of the poet, the beauty of her voice,' for ideals are stirred into life through the poet's lines, which awaken desire and high thoughts. The story has a nobler mission than ever before, because of our need of ideals, of patriotism, of service and of brotherhood.[5]

1. The Western New York Kindergarten Planning Committee, "How Can Teachers, Parents and Administrators Work Together to Develop a Better Understanding of a Good Kindergarten Program?" *The Western New York School Study Quarterly*, XVI (December 1964), 7-9.

2. Margaret Lipchik, "A Saturday School for Mothers and Pre-Schoolers," *The National Elementary Principal*, XLIV (November 1964); Shirley Feldmann, "A Pre-School Enrichment Program for Disadvantaged Children," *The New Era*, XLV (1964), 3.

3. Stephen Dellaquilla, "The Montessori Method," *Research and the Classroom Teacher*, (March 1966), 3-6; Paul W. Blakely and Emma L. Shadle, "A Study of Two Readiness for Reading Programs in Kindergarten," *Elementary English*, XXXVIII (November 1961), 502-505; Nila Banton Smith, "Shall We Teach Formal Reading in the Kindergarten?" *The Compass* (February 1964), 1-8; George D. Spache and Evelyn B. Spache, *Reading in the Elementary School*, Second Edition (Boston: Allyn and Bacon, 1969), 50-52, 59-61.

4. Julius B. Richmond, "Communities in Action: A Report on Project Head Start," *The Reading Teacher*, XIX (February 1966), 323-331.

5. Lucy Wheelock, "Ideas and Ideals," *Readings from Childhood Education* (Washington, D.C.: Association for Childhood Education International, 1966), 283.

BIBLIOGRAPHIC ESSAY

Manuscript Sources

The Sarah Cooper Papers at the Collection of Regional History and University Archives at Cornell University in Ithaca, New York, consists of thirty-two boxes of valuable incoming correspondence, copies of the Jackson Street and Golden Gate Kindergarten Association Annual Reports from 1879-1895, photographs, manuscript copies of speeches and articles, and a few letters from Sarah to her daughter Harriet. The Harriet Skilton Papers in the same archives contain many precious letters written by Sarah to her sister from the 1870's until her death in 1895 concerning charity kindergartens.

Another major source of information about pioneer kindergarten efforts is the William T. Harris Collection at the Missouri Historical Society in St. Louis, Missouri. There are more than twenty vivid letters from Elizabeth Peabody to Harris written between 1870 and 1880, as well as over one hundred letters from Susan Blow to Harris, only about six of which, written between 1872 and 1879, deal specifically with their interest in kindergartens. The Hitchcock Collection at the Missouri Historical Society contains a letter from 1889 reflecting on the state of kindergartens in St. Louis after Susan Blow left, while the Hitchcock Collection in the St. Louis Public Library has several letters written by Miss Blow to Mrs. Henry Hitchcock, apparently an old family friend. Useful letters written by Elizabeth Peabody may be found in the Schlesinger Library at Radcliffe College in Cambridge, Massachusetts, and in the Boston Public Library. Only one of the twenty-three letters written by Miss Peabody in the Boston Public Library pertains to kindergartens, but it clearly reveals the author's ideas about teacher training and the meaning of being a kindergartner.

In Washington, D.C., the archives of the Association of Childhood Education International, originally known as the International Kindergarten Union, contain many materials of inestimable worth to the researcher, including a set of Froebel's gifts made by the Milton Bradley Company, a school diary kept by Elizabeth Harrison, numerous cutting, weaving, folding, and sewing books, as well as notebooks from women attending training schools, and a wealth of correspondence from Susan Blow to Fanniebelle Curtis, mainly dating from the controversial years when they were members of the I.K.U. Committee of Nineteen.

The William F. Mason Papers at the Minnesota Historical Society include Rachel Mason's kindergarten lesson plan book. The Gibson-Humphrey Papers at the University of Kentucky's Margaret I. King Library have eleven letters written to Mrs. Humphrey about kindergartens in Versailles, Kentucky. The Manuscript Division of the Library of Congress in Washington, D.C., has two collections of varying interest to the researcher. The Maria Kraus-Boelte Collection is skimpy, but the William Howard Taft Family Papers have interesting correspondence to and from the President's mother, who was instrumental in starting the Cincinnati Free Kindergarten Association in 1879. Finally, single pertinent letters may be found in the Lillian D. Wald Papers at the New York Public Library and in the Blaine Papers at the State Historical Society of Wisconsin.

Books on Froebel and the Kindergarten

There are several books translating Friedrich Froebel's writings. William Hailmann translated Froebel's *The Education of Man* (New York: D. Appleton & Co., 1904); Josephine Jarvis did *The Pedagogics of the Kindergarten* (New York: D. Appleton & Co., 1897); and Miss Jarvis also helped Fannie E. Dwight translate *Mother-Play and Nursery Songs* (Boston: Lothrop, Lee & Shepard Co., 1906). All three are thorough and complete, but the writing is often involuted and difficult to read. Irene M. Lilley's book *Friedrich Froebel* (Cambridge, England: Cambridge University Press, 1967) translates sections of Froebel's writings in lucid, modern day English. Two good books containing translations of letters are Arnold H. Heinemann,

Froebel's Letters (Boston: Lothrop, Lee & Shepard Co., 1893), and Emilie Michaelis and H. Keatley Moore, *Autobiography of Friedrich Froebel* (Syracuse: C. W. Bardeen Co., 1889).

In addition to translations, there were many books published explaining the kindergarten program. Inasmuch as they reflect slight variations of approach, most of the following proved useful:

Blow, Susan E. *Educational Issues in the Kindergarten.* New York: D. Appleton & Co., 1908.

———*Mottoes and Commentaries of Friedrich Froebel's Mother-Play.* New York: D. Appleton and Co., 1895.

———*Letters to a Mother on the Philosophy of Froebel.* New York: D. Appleton and Co., 1900.

———*Symbolic Education.* New York: D. Appleton and Co., 1894.

Douai, Adolf. *The Kindergarten: A Manual for the Introduction of Froebel's System of Primary Education.* New York: E. Steiger, 1871.

Four Active Workers. *The Kindergarten and the School.* Springfield, Massachusetts: M. Bradley Co., 1886.

Hailmann, William N. *Kindergarten Culture in the Family and Kindergarten.* New York: D. Appleton and Co., 1873.

Harrison, Elizabeth A. *A Study of Child Nature From the Kindergarten Standpoint.* Chicago: Chicago Kindergarten College, 1900.

Hughes, James L. *Froebel's Education Laws for all Teachers.* New York: D. Appleton and Co., 1907.

International Kindergarten Union Committee of Nineteen. *The Kindergarten.* Boston: Houghton Mifflin, 1913.

Kraus-Boelte, Maria and John Kraus. *The Kindergarten Guide*, 2 vols. New York: E. Steiger and Co., 1877.

Peabody, Elizabeth Palmer. *Lectures in the Training Schools for Kindergartners.* Boston: D.C. Heath and Co., 1897.

Pollock, Louise (Mrs.) *National Kindergarten Manual.* Boston: Lee and Shepard Co., 1889.

Shirreff, Emily. *The Kinder-garten at Home.* London: J. Hughes, 1884.

Wiebe, Edward. *The Paradise of Childhood*, Quarter Century Edition. Springfield, Massachusetts: M. Bradley Co., 1896.

Wiggin, Kate D. and Nora A. Smith. *The Republic of Childhood*, 3 vols. Boston: Houghton Mifflin Co., 1896.

Biographical Materials

There are only a few biographies written about kindergartners. Ruth M. Baylor, *Elizabeth Palmer Peabody: Kindergarten Pioneer* (Philadelphia: University of Pennsylvania Press, 1965) is a scholarly analysis. Marguerite N. Bell's *With Banners: A Biography of Stella L. Wood* (St. Paul, Minnesota: Macalester College Press, 1954) is helpful, as is Fletcher Swift's brief *Emma Marwedel: Pioneer of the Kindergarten in California* (University of California Publications in Education, Vol. VI, 1930-1932). Biographical sketches of several kindergartners can be found in the *Dictionary of American Biography*, 12 vols. (New York: Charles Scribner's Sons); in the International Kindergarten Union Committee of Nineteen, *Pioneers of the Kindergarten in America* (New York, 1924); in the more recent *Notable American Women, 1607-1950*, 3 vols. (Cambridge: Harvard University Press, Belknap Press, 1971); and in Kate Douglas Wiggin's *My Garden of Memory: An Autobiography* (Boston: Houghton Mifflin Co., 1923) which is a well-written, delightful account of the author's life and work as a kindergartner. Jack K. Campbell, *Colonel Francis W. Parker: Children's Crusader* (New York: Teachers College Press, 1967) is a fine analysis and sheds light on the development of progressive education in the last quarter of the nineteenth century as well as on Parker's role in the kindergarten movement. Denton J. Snider's *The Life of Friedrich Froebel* (Chicago: Sigma Publishing Co., 1900) is adequate, while Baroness Marenholtz-Bulow's *Reminiscences of Friedrich Froebel* (New York: C.T. Dillingham, 1877), translated by Mary Mann, remains the best biography of Froebel.

Periodical Literature

The yearly volumes of the *National Educational Association Journal of Proceedings and Addresses* contain numerous articles about kindergartens as early as 1877. In 1884, the N.E.A. added a kindergarten department which became a kind of national forum for those involved in the kindergarten movement. A few of the numerous significant articles include: Anna E. Bryan, "The Letter Killeth," (1890), 573-581; William N. Hailmann, "Schoolishness in the Kindergarten," (1890), 565-573; and Francis W. Parker, "The Child," (1889), 479-482.

The "Kindergarten and Child Culture Papers," published in

Henry Barnard's *American Journal of Education*, XXX (1881), are extremely valuable articles, and they deal with various aspects of the early kindergarten movement. See, for example, Thomas Hunter, "The Kindergarten in Normal Training," 197-200, and Reverend R. Heber Newton, "The Free Kindergarten in Church Work," 705-30. *Education, Educational Review, Elementary School Teacher*, the *Yearbooks* of the National Society for the Scientific Study of Education, the *New England Journal of Education, The Pedagogical Seminary, Teachers College Record*, and the *Wisconsin Journal of Education*, all published valuable articles on the kindergarten including:

Butler, Nicholas Murray, "Some Criticism of the Kindergarten," *Educational Review*, XVIII (October 1899), 285-291.

Eby, Frederick, "The Reconstruction of the Kindergarten," *The Pedagogical Seminary*, VII (1900), 229-286.

Grace, Owen, "A Study of the Original Kindergartens," *Elementary School Teacher*, VII (December 1906), 202-213.

Hall, G. Stanley, "The Content of Children's Minds on Entering School," *Pedagogical Seminary*, I (1891), 139-173.

Hill, Patty Smith, "Some Conservative and Progressive Phases of Kindergarten Education," *National Society for the Scientific Study of Education Sixth Yearbook*, Part II (1907), 61-85.

Hervey, Walter L., "Historical Sketch of Teachers College," *Teachers College Record*, IV (November 1903), 45-76.

Kirkpatrick, Edwin A. "The Psychologic Basis of the Kindergarten," *National Society for the Scientific Study of Education Sixth Yearbook*, Part II (1907), 19-31.

Peabody, Elizabeth Palmer, "The Origin and Growth of the Kindergarten," *Education*, II (May-June 1882), 507-527.

Ryan, Mary, "A Garden Where Children Grow," *Wisconsin Journal of Education*, LXXXVI (November 1953), 6-9+.

Thorndike, Edward L., "Notes on Psychology for Kindergartners," *Teachers College Record*, IV (November 1903), 45-76.

Vandewalker, Nina C. "The History of Kindergarten Influence in Elementary Education," *National Society for the Scientific Study of Education Sixth Yearbook*, Part II (1907), 115-133.

In addition, there were a few publications devoted only to the kindergarten. Elizabeth Peabody's *The Kindergarten Messenger*, first printed in 1873, merged in 1877 to be called *The New Educa-*

tion. Kindergarten News was published for several years beginning in 1890 in Buffalo, New York. *Kindergarten Review* started about the same time as the *News*, but ceased publication in 1915, and reemerged later first called *Kindergarten and First Grade* and then *American Childhood. The Kindergarten*, which began publication in 1888 and ceased in 1933, probably had the widest circulation of any of the kindergarten periodicals. Its pages recorded and discussed events significant to and the growth and development of the kindergarten movement. The articles, however, were by and large written by insiders to an audience of insiders. The journal changed its name to *The Kindergarten Magazine* in 1891, to *The Kindergarten Magazine and Pedagogical Digest* in 1906, and finally to *Kindergarten-Primary Magazine* in 1907.

Several other journals besides those devoted exclusively to educational matters published articles that proved useful in this research. Marion Carter's "The Kindergarten Child—After the Kindergarten," appeared in the *Atlantic Monthly*, LXXXIII (March 1899), 358-366. *Century Magazine* had assorted items on the kindergartens, especially during the 1890's when the editor, Richard Watson Gilder, was also President of the New York Kindergarten Association. *The Charities Review, Forum, Lend a Hand, Home Mission Monthly, The New Cycle, The Outlook, The Overland Monthly, Social Progress*, and *Survey Graphic* were also useful. *The Ladies Home Journal* published a five-part series by Nora A. Smith called "The Kindergarten Possible to Every Home and Village," from November, 1898, to March, 1899. Finally, the *Proceedings of the National Conference on Charities and Corrections* provided a wealth of information on charity kindergartens in the 1880's and 1890's. See, for example, Sarah B. Cooper, "The Kindergarten as a Child-Saving Work" (1882), 130-138; Constance MacKenzie, "Charity and the Kindergarten" (1886), 48-53; the Reverend R. Heber Newton, "The Bearing of the Kindergarten on the Prevention of Crime" (1886), 53-58; and Kate Douglas Wiggin, "The Relation of the Kindergarten to Social Reform" (1888), 247-258.

The *Bulletins* and *Circulars* issued by the United States Bureau of Education are other forms of worthwhile periodical literature. Three that were most helpful are: *Kindergartens in the United States* (Bulletin no. 6, 1914); Luella A. Palmer, *Adjustment Between Kindergarten and First Grade* (Bulletin no. 24, 1915); and Mary G. Waite, *The Kindergarten in Certain School Survey* (Bulletin no. 13, 1926).

Annual Reports

Another important source of information was a scattered assortment of annual reports including those from the Kitchen Garden Association; the Brooklyn, the Louisville, the Elm City, and the Golden Gate Free Kindergarten Associations; the Henshaw Memorial Free Kindergarten; the New York Kindergarten Association; the Silver Street Kindergarten Society; the Pioneer Kindergarten Society of San Francisco; and the National Kindergarten Association.

In addition to kindergarten organizations, the annual reports of the United Relief Works of the Society for Ethical Culture, the Hebrew Free School Association, and the Educational Alliance and the *Yearbooks* of St. George's Church in New York City were invaluable. So, too, were the annual reports of school superintendents in such cities as St. Louis, New York City, Cincinnati, Boston, Newton, Massachusetts, and Baltimore, and in such states as Illinois and New York.

Finally, the *Reports of the United States Commissioner of Education* provided a great deal of information regarding the growth and extension of Froebel's system. Laura Fisher's "The Kindergarten" published in the 1903 *Report*, vol. I, 689-719, was particularly helpful.

Relevant Books

Nina C. Vandewalker's, *The Kindergarten in American Education* (New York: The Macmillan Co., 1908), is essentially a chronology without identified sources held together by a few interpretive comments. Nina Vandewalker was a kindergartner intricately bound up in many of the events she described, and her writing reflects clear biases. Evelyn Weber's *The Kindergarten* (New York: Teachers College Press, 1969) is devoted largely to the development of the modern kindergarten program and curriculum with only a section on the early history of the kindergarten movement based on published source materials.

While most of the kindergarten literature, other than the books explaining Froebel's programs, tended to be in the form of articles, some books were helpful in analyzing the effect of the kindergarten on education generally. These include John Dewey, *The School and Society* (Chicago: University of Chicago Press, 1956); John and

113

Evelyn Dewey, *Schools of Tomorrow* (New York: Dutton, 1962); the first chapter of G. Stanley Hall, *Educational Problems*, vol. I (New York: D. Appleton and Co., 1911); Frederic and Caroline Burk, *A Study of the Kindergarten Problem in the Public Kindergartens of Santa Barbara, California, 1898-1899* (New York: Teachers College Press, 1920); Olive Russell and Alice O'Grady, *Gateways to Art and Industry* (Springfield: M. Bradley and Co., 1913); Tsunekichi Mizuno, *The Kindergarten in Japan* (Boston: The Stratford Co., 1917); and Michael Anagnos, *Kindergarten and Primary School for the Blind* (Boston: Franklin Press, 1886).

In studying the origins of Teachers College, Columbia, Lawrence Cremin, David Shanon, and Mary Townsend, *A History of Teachers College, Columbia University* (New York: Columbia University Press, 1954), and James Earl Russell's *Founding Teachers College* (New York: Columbia University Press, 1937), are informative and useful, but it is helpful to go back to Emily Huntington's *The Kitchen Garden* (New York: Schermerhorn Co., 1878), and *How to Teach Kitchen Garden* (New York: Doubleday, Page & Co., 1901); Columbia University Teachers College *Announcements*; and an address given in 1927 at the fortieth anniversary luncheon of the Horace Mann School by Nicholas Murray Butler entitled "The Origins of Teachers College and the Horace Mann School."

There are several general works on the history of women in America, although none discuss the career of kindergartening in particular. Some of the better sources include: Andrew Sinclair, *The Better Half: The Emancipation of the American Woman* (New York: Harper & Row, 1965); Robert A. Smuts, *Women and Work in America* (New York: Columbia University Press, 1959); Aileen S. Kraditor, editor, *Up From the Pedestal* (Chicago: Quadrangle Books, 1968); Eleanor Flexner, *Century of Struggle: The Woman's Rights Movement in the United States* (Cambridge, Massachusetts: Belknap Press, 1959); Robert E. Riegel, *American Feminists* (Lawrence, Kansas: University of Kansas Press, 1963); and Barbara Welter, "The Cult of True Womanhood, 1820-1860," *American Quarterly* (Summer, 1966), Part I, 151-174. Frances Willard and Mary Livermore, editors, *A Woman of the Century* (Buffalo: C. W. Moulton, 1893), is an encyclopedia of short biographies of women with only a few kindergartners entered. Thomas Woody's *History of Women's Education in the United States* (New York: Science Press, 1929), 2 vols., has a good section on women in the teaching profession. George S.

114

Counts, *School and Society in Chicago* (New York: Harcourt, Brace & Co., 1928), has a chapter on the educational work of women's clubs; and Catherine Filene, editor, *Careers for Women* (Boston: Houghton Mifflin Co., 1920), is a vocational guide which includes information on becoming a kindergartner.

There are many accounts that give the reader an understanding of turn-of-the-century urban problems and various attempts at social reform. Autobiographies like William S. Rainsford, *The Story of a Varied Life* (New York: Doubleday, Page and Co., 1922); Lillian D. Wald, *The House on Henry Street* (New York: Henry Holt and Co., 1915); and Jane Addams, *Twenty Years at Hull House* (New York: The Macmillan Co., 1910), and *Second Twenty Years at Hull House* (New York: The Macmillan Co., 1930), give the reader insights into personal crusades, while Robert A. Woods and Albert J. Kennedy, *The Settlement Horizon* (New York: Russell Sage Foundation, 1922), and Woods and Kennedy, editors, *Handbook of Settlements* (New York: Charities Publication Committee, 1911), give a more precise idea of the role of the kindergarten in social settlements. Books like John Spargo, *The Bitter Cry of the Children* (New York: The Macmillan Co., 1906, reissued by Quadrangle Books, 1968), and Jacob Riis, *The Children of the Poor* (New York: Charles Scribner's Sons, 1892), describe some of the horrors and discomforts of the impoverished in urban areas, dwelling mainly upon the children as unfortunate victims.

General Works

There are several general interpretative works on late nineteenth and early twentieth century educational and social reform which are thought-provoking and essential to our understanding of the period. With the exception of Timothy L. Smith's short but provocative article, "Progressivism in American Education, 1880-1900," *Harvard Educational Review*, XXX (Spring, 1961), 168-193, most unfortunately do not include the role of the kindergarten movement in their analyses, and if they do treat the subject, it is tangentially. The following selected general works, however, proved helpful:

Abell, Aaron. *The Urban Impact on American Protestantism, 1865-1900.* Cambridge, Massachusetts: Harvard University Press, 1943.

Bremner, Robert H. *From the Depths*. New York: New York University Press, 1964.

Chambers, Clarke A. *Seedtime of Reform*. Minneapolis: University of Minnesota Press, 1963. Especially chapter 2.

Cohen, Sol. *Progressives and Urban School Reform*. New York: Bureau of Publications, Teachers College, Columbia University, 1964.

Cremin, Lawrence A. *The Transformation of the School*. New York: A. Knopf, 1961.

Davis, Allen F. *Spearheads for Reform*. New York: Oxford University Press, 1967.

Handlin, Oscar. *John Dewey's Challenge to Education*. New York: Harper, 1959.

———*The Uprooted*. Boston: Little, Brown, and Co., 1951.

Lubove, Roy. *The Professional Altruist: The Emergence of Social Work as a Career, 1880-1930*. Cambridge: Harvard University Press, 1965.

May, Henry F. *Protestant Churches and Industrial America*. New York: Octagon Books, 1963.

Rischin, Moses. *The Promised City: New York's Jews, 1870-1914*. Cambridge, Massachusetts: Harvard University Press, 1962.

Strickland, Charles and Charles Burgess, editors. *Health, Heredity, and Growth: G. Stanley Hall on Natural Education*. New York: Teachers College Press, 1965.

Timberlake, James H. *Prohibition and the Progressive Movement, 1900-1920*. Cambridge, Massachusetts: Harvard University Press, 1963.

Wade, Louise C. *Graham Taylor: Pioneer for Social Justice, 1851-1938*. Chicago: University of Chicago Press, 1964.

Wishy, Bernard. *The Child and the Republic*. Philadelphia: University of Pennsylvania Press, 1968.

INDEX

117

119